Families

A Handbook of
Concepts and Techniques
for the
Helping Professional

Families

A Handbook of Concepts and Techniques for the Helping Professional

Kenneth Davis

Villanova University

Brooks/Cole Publishing Company

I(T)P™ An International Thomson Publishing Company

Pacific Grove • Albany • Bonn • Boston • Cincinnati • Detroit • London • Madrid • Melbourne
Mexico City • New York • Paris • San Francisco • Singapore • Tokyo • Toronto • Washington

A CLAIREMONT BOOK

Sponsoring Editor: *Claire Verduin*
Marketing Representative: *Ronald E. Shelley*
Editorial Associate: *Patsy Vienneau*
Production Editor: *Penelope Sky*
Production Assistant: *Dorothy Bell*
Manuscript Editor: *Catherine Cambron*
Permissions Editor: *Cathleen S. Collins*

Interior and Cover Design: *Terri Wright*
Art Coordinator: *Lisa Torri*
Interior Illustration: *Lisa Torri*
Typesetting: *Bookends Typesetting*
Cover Printing: *Phoenix Color Corporation, Inc.*
Printing and Binding: *Quebecor/Fairfield*

All cartoons courtesy of David Mio Huth.

For more information, contact:

BROOKS/COLE PUBLISHING COMPANY
511 Forest Lodge Road
Pacific Grove, CA 93950
USA

International Thomson Publishing Europe
Berkshire House 168–173
High Holborn
London WC1V 7AA
England

Thomas Nelson Australia
102 Dodds Street
South Melbourne, 3205
Victoria, Australia

Nelson Canada
1120 Birchmount Road
Scarborough, Ontario
Canada M1K 5G4

International Thomson Editores
Campos Eliseos 385, Piso 7
Col. Polanco
11560 México D. F. México

International Thomson Publishing GmbH
Königswinterer Strasse 418
53227 Bonn
Germany

International Thomson Publishing Asia
221 Henderson Road
#05–10 Henderson Building
Singapore 0315

International Thomson Publishing Japan
Hirakawacho Kyowa Building, 3F
2-2-1 Hirakawacho
Chiyoda-ku, Tokyo 102
Japan

Printed in the United States of America.

10   9   8   7   6   5   4   3   2   1

Library of Congress Cataloging-in-Publication Data

Davis, Kenneth
    Families : a handbook of concepts and techniques for the helping
professional / Kenneth Davis.
        p. cm.
    Includes bibliographical references.
    ISBN 0-534-25806-9
    1. Family psychotherapy   I. Title.
RC488.5.D36   1995
616.89'156—dc20   95-2878
                                              CIP

To our families

John and Mildred Burns
Kenneth and Dorothy Davis

KENNETH DAVIS is a member of the faculty of Villanova University and maintains a private practice in psychology. During the past twenty-five years he has also been a school counselor, a couples' therapist, and a children's counselor. He has been recognized by the Pennsylvania Counseling Association and the Pennsylvania School Counselor Association. Dr. Davis makes frequent workshop presentations and is a consultant to numerous organizations.

Preface

This book is for students and practitioners who are interested in or currently working with families. Because families differ so greatly, the professional helper should be able to choose from numerous possible interventions to help all family members learn about themselves cognitively, affectively, and behaviorally.

In three main sections are the following features:

- *concepts* that therapists can use to help families understand themselves
- a wide variety of *techniques* that will help families apply their understanding
- *worksheets* that help families respond more fully to the intervention, and *guidelines* to benefit therapists

The concepts, techniques, and worksheets are interdependent. Techniques allow the concepts to be developed not only in the mind but also in actual behavior. Throughout the text, I have used the fictional Evans family to show the practical effects of intervention. The Evanses are a blended, conjoint family, which allows the helping professional to examine the widest possible variety of interventions in relation to a single case example.

Acknowledgments
Many of the concepts, techniques, worksheets, and guidelines came from well-known family therapists who have both practiced and written extensively. They are acknowledged specifically in the text.

Barbara Serratore enthusiastically organized the numerous tasks necessary to completing this project. Gary English developed many of the worksheets and guidelines. Joyce Lynn Spenard gave invaluable input on the presentation of concepts, and also checked references. Elizabeth J. Landis patiently transformed most of the text into electronic format. Many current and former students, especially in my family therapy classes, provided encouragement and ideas.

I express my gratitude to my editor, Claire Verduin, for the opportunity to publish this book, and to her staff, especially Penelope Sky, for transforming a rough manuscript into a book. The following reviewers offered helpful comments and suggestions: Clarence Hibbs, Pepperdine University; Lynda Kayser, Eastern Illinois University; Vincent D. Foley, Long Island University–C.W. Post; Uri Ruveni, University of Houston; and Mary Sferre, University of North Florida.

I am indebted to my family for their support and to families in therapy for the experience they have provided.

Kenneth Davis

Families

A Handbook of
Concepts and Techniques
for the
Helping Professional

INTRODUCTION

THE FAMILY STRUCTURE

Every family creates a structure that allows them to function. This structure can lead to the family becoming a smooth functioning unit or a harmful dysfunctional unit that ultimately leads to dysfunctional individuals. Many factors contribute to a family's structure: the mother's and father's families of origin; the relationship of mother and father; the family's financial resources; and the family's religious beliefs. Three concepts are helpful in considering these factors: roles, rules, and expectations. The family must be able to discern and agree on its overt roles, rules, and expectations. In addition, roles, rules, and expectations held by individuals but not revealed to the rest of the family need to be examined. These covert concepts are often a family's stumbling block, because most family members truly do not know why so much conflict goes on in the family. Each of these three concepts will be examined in more detail.

Roles are the defined and accepted set of responsibilities for each family member. In every culture, roles are defined in part by the jobs one performs. Because of woman's ability to bear children, man's role became that of provider. In our culture, women have traditionally been caregivers whose job has been to care for children and home. Both parents traditionally were involved in nurturing and training children, since the father and the extended family were usually close at hand. For some families in every culture, roles are defined by religious beliefs.

The provider role changed significantly during the industrial revolution, when men who had traditionally worked near home suddenly began working longer days and longer weeks away from home. As a result, men's and women's roles became even more distinct. As goods and housing became more plentiful, and with the decline of multigenerational households, more pressure was put on both caregiver and provider.

Children's roles historically have been to play at being adults. Although many cultures teach children to honor and obey their parents, in all cultures children learn by mimicking adults. If you doubt this fact, stick out your tongue at a toddler. Watch a two-year-old pretending to cook like mommy or daddy, or a four-year-old following parents as they do their chores and helping by handing out tools from the toolbox.

Roles have been passed down from generation to generation. Roles in recent decades, however, have changed drastically. With women in the workforce in record numbers, our society is moving toward a more equal sharing of the responsibilities involved in the jobs that define our roles. Today's high divorce rate, resulting in increasing numbers of single-parent families, has created a society where preconceived roles no longer apply. Life in the family has therefore become much more confusing for parents and children.

Rules are the overt or covert regulations that help family members interact. These general guidelines convey the mores of interpersonal relationships, such as what is acceptable behavior and what procedures are appropriate in various situations. Rules tend to change or evolve as the family matures. Many rules are brought into a marriage from the husband's and the wife's families of origin, and these rules help the family maintain order while it develops the rules it will follow as a new family. These inherent rules are usually the covert ones, unspoken social mores that guide behavior: a wife may give her husband time he needs to unwind after work, or a husband may know when to take the kids out for a walk. A more directly inherited rule is "My parents did it this way so that's how I do it."

Then there are overt rules, which a family makes together. Though their parents did things differently, the new couple chooses their own path and makes their own rules. These rules tend to evolve as the marriage and family grows and develops. Because overt rules are less entrenched and have been formulated consciously, they are somewhat easier to change than the unconsciously adopted covert rules.

Finally, there are rules for making more rules. These meta-rules help the family to make and enforce rules. Meta-rules concern decisions about which rules are important and who is going to develop and enforce them.

Expectations come into the marriage or family situation not only as ghosts from the past, but also as individual personality preferences. Expectations concern what individuals anticipate or feel is due them as their right.

Internal expectations come from a person's family of origin and from life experience. Based on individual values and belief systems, internal expectations can be conscious or unconscious, rooted in reality or unrealistic. For example, if a husband expects his wife to be as overtly affectionate as he is, he has an internal expectation. These internal expectations often are unstated or assumed, and thus often cause conflict in a relationship.

In addition to internal expectations, society places external expectations on couples. Families and friends—as well as the surrounding community and culture—all place expectations on a couple or family. An example of these expectations are social reactions to whether a mother stays home with her children or leaves the home to work. Social expectations to some extent are the glue that keeps a society functioning as a whole. They can create excessive pressures, though, for some groups, such as teens and enmeshed families.

Conflicts among roles, rules, and expectations are stumbling blocks to many marriage and family interactions. Understanding each component is vital to understanding how a family functions. Discerning which concepts are in conflict can help families resolve their problems and promote healthy change.

CASE STUDY

The Evans Family

The Evans family consists of Keith Evans; his son and daughter by a former marriage, Keith Jr. and Anita; his present wife Linda; and her two children from a former marriage, Kim and Mark. In addition, Keith and Linda have a five-year-old daughter, Ruth. The Evans family came to therapy on its own initiative. Keith and Linda are concerned about the difficulties they have been having with all the children during the eight years they've been married. Since Keith and Linda married, their former spouses, Ann and Al, have each also remarried. Ann has had a son. There has been very little peace and a consistent pattern of acting-out behavior among the five children during Keith and Linda's marriage.

Evans Family Developmental Genogram

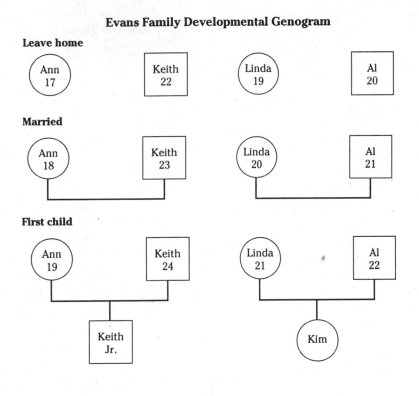

Symbols: ⋀⋀ conflict —╱— separation —╱╱— divorce

**Second child
Separation**

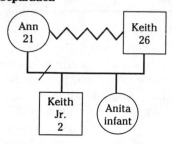

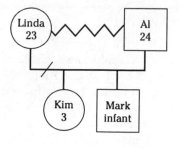

Divorce

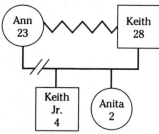

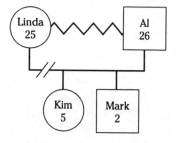

Remarriage

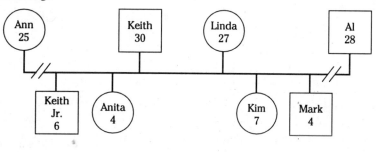

Their first child

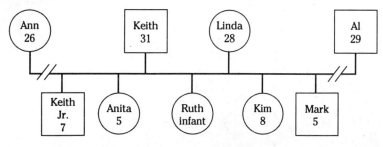

Now

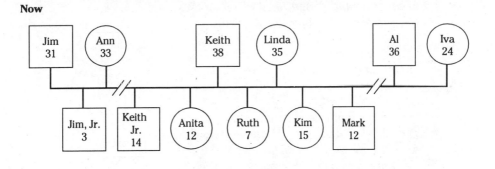

THE EVANS' FAMILY ROLES

Dirty Socks

Family roles are a set of well-defined and accepted responsibilities for the husband, wife, and children. Each generation accepts some roles from the previous generation, while rejecting others. The Evans family is no exception. Its difficulties are compounded because it is a combination of three families, made up of four adults and five children. With four different families of origin, both the parents and the children have many role models to choose from or to be confused by. We will look at the role of responsibility for getting dirty socks clean.

Dirty Socks

Keith was the breadwinner.
His father was a breadwinner.
His mother never worked outside the home.
She took pride in the family's clothes being clean—especially
  their socks.

Ann, Keith's first wife, worked outside the home.
Both her mother and her father worked.
Her mother always did the laundry.
When Ann was twelve, she began doing her own laundry.
She hated doing it, as did her brothers.

Even as a child, Linda liked clean clothes.
Her mother and father did not care.
Neither parent could keep a job.
Clothes were not very important to them.
Linda faithfully washed everyone's clothes.

Al was a clotheshorse.
His parents both liked to buy clothes.
They worked and gave Al any clothes he wanted.
Al rarely washed any of his clothes.
He sometimes wore four outfits in one day.
His family had a maid who washed all their clothes.

Keith and Ann got married.
Keith did not want Ann to work.
Keith wanted Ann to do the laundry.
Ann did it for a while, but she resented it.
She thought Keith should pick up and wash his own socks.

Linda and Al got married.
Both of them had to work to buy a house.
Linda could not believe how many clothes Al had.
She also had more clothes.
She liked to wash their clothes.

Keith and Ann had two children.
Linda and Al had two children.
Who did the laundry became an issue.
Keith demanded that Ann wash the dirty socks.
Al didn't like the way Linda does the laundry.

Keith and Ann are divorced, in part because of dirty socks.
Linda and Al are divorced, not because of dirty socks.
Linda and Keith are married and live with all four children.
They also have Ruth.

Keith is the breadwinner, but needs Linda to work.
Linda believes dirty clothes reflect on her.
She enjoys working so her family can have more clothes.
She washes all fifty pairs of dirty socks each week.
She has accepted washing dirty socks as her role.

Each family develops specific roles for the husband and wife so that they can function together and limit the conflict within the family. As the family changes, with children coming into the family and later leaving, these roles change dramatically. Sometimes, roles change by choice, but most often, they change in response to other changes in the family, which require the couple to modify their roles or else be in conflict. A couple has many choices to make about roles as their children and family grow. As long as the roles and changing roles are accepted by both parents, there will be less conflict and a stable structure for the children.

THE EVANS' FAMILY RULES

Stewed Tomatoes

Family rules are regulations that help the family know how to act and interact within the family. Each member of a couple brings into a marriage many family rules that reflect how their parents did things. These family rules are helpful when they provide a framework for the family to function comfortably. But when a family rule results in serious conflict, the family either discards or ignores the rule, modifies it, or enforces it. Family rules deal with almost every aspect of an individual's life within the family. We will examine how the Evans family arrived at one family rule concerning stewed tomatoes.

Stewed Tomatoes

Keith did not like stewed tomatoes.
His mother and father both liked them.
His mother knew Keith did not like stewed tomatoes.
His parents believed you should eat everything served to you.
His mother never served Keith stewed tomatoes.

Ann, Keith's first wife, liked stewed tomatoes.
Her mother liked stewed tomatoes.
Her father disliked stewed tomatoes.
Her mother became upset when anyone disliked her cooking.
Her father always ate the stewed tomatoes.

Linda really liked stewed tomatoes.
Her mother and father had a huge garden.
They canned hundreds of quarts of tomatoes.
Her family enjoyed eating stewed tomatoes.
They could never understand why people disliked canned tomatoes.

Al, Linda's first husband, hated all vegetables.
His mother and father disagreed about vegetables.
When just his mother was home, Al had to eat them.
He decided he would never eat vegetables as an adult.
When both parents were home, his father did not make Al eat
*   his vegetables.*

Keith and Ann got married.
Ann served Keith stewed tomatoes.
Keith would not eat the stewed tomatoes.
Ann was hurt.
She never served them again to him.

Linda and Al got married.
Linda canned many vegetables from her parents' big garden.
Al would not eat any of these vegetables.
Linda said that he was wasting good food.
She continued to can and eat the vegetables herself.

Ann and Keith had two children, Keith Jr. and Anita.
Ann served stewed tomatoes to the whole family.
But only Keith Jr. would eat them.
Ann hid them in the goulash.
Keith Sr. and Anita still hated them and picked them out.

Al and Linda had two children, Kim and Mark.
Linda still canned vegetables and served them to her family.
Both children like vegetables. Both children like stewed tomatoes.
Al did not eat vegetables and Linda said he was stupid.

Ann and Keith are divorced, not because of stewed tomatoes.
Al and Linda are divorced, in part because of stewed tomatoes.
Keith and Linda are married and have custodial care of all
    four children.
They also have Ruth.

One night Linda serves stewed tomatoes.
Keith Sr. does not make the children eat the stewed tomatoes.
Linda tries serving stewed tomatoes once a month anyway.
Only Keith Jr. enjoys the stewed tomatoes.

Anita has never even tried stewed tomatoes.
Kim sometimes eats stewed tomatoes but does not eat any
    other vegetables.
Mark eats everything put in front of him.
Ruth doesn't eat much of anything anytime.

While it is not clear what the rules are or who made them,
there are maybe seven stewed tomato rules in the Evans family—or
    maybe there is no stewed tomato rule at all.

Parents do provide rules for their children. Blended families have difficulties making family rules, and need to be able to function more comfortably within agreed-upon family rules. Most of the many rules that families have to work out concern matters that are more complex than stewed tomatoes. Therapists must track family rules and assess their significance. Therapists must also examine the rules that they themselves bring to a session and acknowledge the impact these rules can have on the family.

THE EVANS' FAMILY EXPECTATION: SECURITY

Family expectations involve what family members anticipate as their due, as necessary, as proper, or as what they are looking forward to. Each member of a family expects something from other members of the family. Husbands and wives expect their spouses to meet some of their needs. Children expect their parents to love them. Many parents expect children to obey them. Everyone enters into marriage with some expectations. We will examine some expectations of the Evans family.

Security

Keith had expected his wife to be a housewife.
Ann, Keith's first wife, had expected wealth.
Linda had expected to have a house and children.
Al, Linda's first husband, had expected to have what he wanted.

Keith and Ann married.
Ann wanted to work so they could have more.
When the children came along, Ann's dream faded.
As Ann became disenchanted, Keith became disgusted.
Keith and Ann divorced.

Linda and Al married.
Both worked to have the house Linda wanted and the clothes and
    status Al wanted.
As children arrived, Al and Linda lost their house because Linda
    could not work.
Linda and Al divorced.

After a time Keith, who had a house and wanted a wife,
    married Linda.
They had one more child together.
Keith and Linda expected all the children to be happy now that
    their own expectations were met.

Because each member of the family has his or her own set of expectations, a family therapist needs to help each individual become aware of and begin to understand what he or she expects from every other member of the family. This awareness will require many different kinds of interventions.

THE CONNECTION

This handbook has been designed to give you a resource to use while working with families. Students in training as well as practitioners of family therapy will be able to benefit from this handbook. The book's three cross-referenced sections cover **concepts** (ideas for families to learn); **techniques** (activities for families to do); and **guidelines** with worksheets. For each of the concepts listed, three related techniques are suggested, but by no means are they the only ones available. Feel free to use whatever works for you. The techniques often have corresponding worksheets or guidelines, which help clarify how to proceed.

Original sources of the concepts and techniques have been identified so that those desiring more detail can obtain additional information. Also, a brief overview and an initial statement that the therapist can use are provided. The last section of the book consists of guidelines and worksheets that can be used in conjunction with a technique. These are identified with specific techniques but may be used independently.

The author's experience is that most families are exhausted by the lack of knowledge about what is happening to them and why. This book attempts to share concepts and techniques from a wide variety of approaches to family therapy and to show how these concepts and techniques can be used with families.

THE CONNECTION CHART

continued

THE CONNECTION CHART

PART ONE Concept	PART TWO Techniques	PART THREE Resources
Calibration 36	Restructuring 190 Rules Identification 194 Rules of Interaction 195	Family Reconstruction 253 Rules 267 Meta-Rules 258
Chemical Dependency 37	Challenging the Structure 128 Conflict Management 134 Transactional Patterns 210	Pathway 263 Stances 240 Family Reconstruction 253
Circular Causality 38	Circular Questions 131 Defining the Problem 138 Role Playing 192	Circular Questions 224 Problem Solving 264 Role Playing 237
Circularity 39	Monitoring 168 Pretend 185 Self-Disclosure 197	Journal Format 256 Role Playing 237 Johari Window 255
Closed System 40	Self-Disclosure 197 Storytelling 202 Transactional Patterns 210	Johari Window 255 Self-Disclosure 238 Family Reconstruction 253
Coevolution 41	Boundaries 125 Circular Interview 130 Joining 161	Genogram 231 Circular Questions 224 Self-Disclosure 238
Communication Styles 42	Communication Stances 133 Looking 164 Photos 180	Stances 240 Nonverbal Cues 260 Childhood Memory 244

Complementary
  Relationship 43
	Paradoxical Double
	  Bind 174
	Rules of Interaction 195
	Taking Sides 205
		Johari Window 255
		
		Meta-Rules 258
		Meta-Rules 258

Compliment 44	Communication Game 132 Encouraging 142 Restructuring 190	Communication 225 Encouragment 229 Family Reconstruction 253
Cooperating 45	Conflict Management 134 Family Reconstruction 150 Harmony among Parts 156	Stances 240 Genogram 231 Problem Solving 264
Coping Ability 46	Harmony among Parts 156 Prescribing the Symptom 184 Tickling of Defenses 207	Problem Solving 264 Expectations 251 Nonverbal Cues 260

THE CONNECTION CHART

PART ONE Concept	PART TWO Techniques	PART THREE Resources
Cybernetics 47	Family Drawing 148 Parallel Examples 177 Role Playing 192	Materials 148 Time Cable 270 Role Playing 237
Delegation 48	Crediting 136 Multidirected Partiality 170 Straightforward Directives 203	Time Cable 270 Journal Format 256 Encouragement 229
Developmental Tasks 49	Circular Questions 131 Parallel Examples 177 Time Out 208	Circular Questions 224 Time Cable 270 Time Out 241
Differentiation of Self 50	Looking 164 Telegram 206 Unbalancing 214	Nonverbal Cues 260 Communication Roadblocks 245 Journal Format 256
Discontinuous Change 51	Negotiation 172 Paradoxical Interventions 175 Skeleton Keys 199	Simple Contract 268 Simple Contract 268 Conflict Resolution 247
Discrimination of Differences 52	Circular Questions 131 Defining the Problem 138 Marital Schism 165	Circular Questions 224 Defining the Problem 249 Conflict Resolution 247
Disengagement 53	Homework Prescription 158 Triangles 212 Value Assessment 216	Relabeling 266 Materials 212 Simple Contract 268
Displacement 54	Empty Chair 140 Marital Stalemate 166 Person to Person 179	Empty Chair 228 Marriage Model 257 Encouragement 229
Distance Regulation 55	Ropes 193 Sculpting 196 Vulnerability Contract 218	Materials 193 Psychodrama 235 Vulnerability Contract 272
Distractor Role 56	Communication Game 132 Positive Reinforcement 183 Video Playback 217	Communication 225 Discipline 226, 227 Nonverbal Cues 260
Double Bind 57	Enactment 141 Telegram 206 Worst Alternative 219	Role Playing 237 Communication Roadblocks 245 Problem Solving 264

continued

THE CONNECTION CHART

PART ONE Concept	PART TWO Techniques	PART THREE Resources
Emotional Cutoff 58	Fighting Fair 152 Looking 164 Rules of Interaction 195	Journal Format 256 Nonverbal Cues 260 Meta-Rules 258
Enabling Family 59	Family Council 147 Skeleton Keys 199 Marital Stalemate 166	Family Minutes 252 Conflict Resolution 247 Marriage Model 257
Enmeshment 60	Boundaries 125 "I" Statements 160 Sociogram 200	Genogram 231 Communication Roadblocks 245 Psychodrama 235
Entitlement 61	Formula Task 154 Motivation 169 Past Successes 178	Observation 261 Conflict Resolution 247 Problem Solving 264
Exoneration 62	Childhood Home 129 Family Secrets 151 Formula Task 154	Childhood Memory 244 Nonverbal Cues 260 Observation 261
Family Life Cycle 63	Encouraging 142 Genogram 155 Typical Day 213	Encouragement 229 Genogram 231 Typical Day Journal 271
Family Pet 64	Encouraging 142 Monitoring 168 Triangles 212	Encouragement 229 Journal Format 256 Materials 212
Family Myths 65	Family Secrets 151 Homework Prescriptions 158 Reframing 188	Nonverbal Cues 260 Relabeling 266 Relabeling 266
Family Structure 66	Rules Identification 194 Rules of Interaction 195 Tickling of Defenses 207	Meta-Rules 258 Meta-Rules and Rules 258, 267 Nonverbal Cues 260
Feedback Loops 67	Communication Stances 133 Harmony among Parts 156 Positive Connotations 181	Stances 240 Problem Solving 264 Meta-Rules 258
First-Order Change 68	Challenging the Communication 127 Formula Task 154 Parallel Examples 177	Communication 225 Observation 261 Time Cable 270

THE CONNECTION CHART

PART ONE Concept	PART TWO Techniques	PART THREE Resources
Forgiveness 69	Empty Chair 140 Encouraging 142 Homework 157	Empty Chair 228 Encouragement 229 Time Cable 270
Fusion 70	Childhood Home 129 Encouraging a Response 143 Value Assessment 216	Childhood Memory 244 Encouragement 229 Expectations 251
Helpfulness as Power 71	Family Reconstruction 150 Quid pro Quo 187 Use of Self 215	Genogram 231 Quid pro Quo Cards 265 Johari Window 255
Homeostasis 72	Expectations Game 144 Reframing 188 Value Assessment 216	Expectations 251 Relabeling 266 Expectations 251
Humor 73	Humor Applied 159 Storytelling 202 Use of Self 215	Humor 233 Self-Disclosure 238 Johari Window 255
Identified Patient 74	Circular Interview 130 Family Secrets 151 Telegram 206	Circular Questions 224 Nonverbal Cues 260 Communication Roadblocks 245
Incongruent Communication 75	Dealing with Anger 137 Empty Chair 140 Worst Alternative 219	Anger 242 Empty Chair 228 Problem Solving 264
Incongruous Dual Hierarchy 76	Reframing 188 Taking Sides 205 Transactional Patterns 210	Relabeling 266 Meta-Rules 258 Family Reconstruction 253
Interface Phenomena 77	Boundaries 125 Motivation 169 Restructuring 190	Genogram 231 Conflict Resolution 247 Family Reconstruction 253
Interpersonal Functions 78	Boundaries 125 Reframing 188 Ropes 193	Genogram 231 Relabeling 266 Materials 193
Introjections 79	Childhood Home 129 Live History 162 Speaker's Chair 201	Childhood Memory 244 Childhood Memory 244 Conflict Resolution 247

continued

THE CONNECTION CHART

PART ONE Concept	PART TWO Techniques	PART THREE Resources
Ledger of Justice 80	Monitoring 168 Person to Person 179 Vulnerability Contract 218	Journal Format 256 Encouragement 229 Vulnerability Contract 272
Loyalty 81	Awareness Enhancement 122 Caring Days 126 Harmony among Parts 156	Childhood Memory 244 Role Playing 237 Childhood Memory 244
Maturation 82	"I" Statements 160 Self-Disclosure 197 Siding 198	Simple Contract 268 Johari Window 255 Dimensions of Support 250
Merited Trustworthiness 83	Crediting 136 Motivation 169 Value Assessment 216	Time Cable 270 Conflict Resolution 247 Expectations 251
Metacommunication 84	Communication Game 132 Rules Identification 194 Rules of Interaction 195	Communication Skills 245 Meta-Rules 258 Journal Format 256
Multigenerational Transmission 85	Childhood Home 129 Expectations Game 144 Systemic Hypothesis 204	Communication 225 Johari Window 255 Circular Questions 224
Mystification 86	Positive Reinforcement 183 Unbalancing 214 Video Playback 217	Communication Roadblocks 245 Rules 267 Meta-Rules 258
Nuclear Family Emotional System 87	Enactment 141 Metaphor 167 Sociogram 200	Role Playing 237 Monitoring 259 Psychodrama 235
Object Relations 88	Childhood Home 129 Enactment 141 Live History 162	Childhood Memory 244 Expectations 251 Genogram 231
Paradigms 89	Bathroom Procedure 123 Homework 157 Rules Identification 194	Discipline 226, 227 Time Cable 270 Journal Format 256
Parentification 90	Boundaries 125 Defining the Problem 138 Pretend 185	Genogram 231 Problem Solving 264 Role Playing 237

THE CONNECTION CHART

PART ONE Concept	PART TWO Techniques	PART THREE Resources
Parts to Be Played 91	Anatomy of a Relationship 121 Sculpting 196 Systemic Hypothesis 204	Role Playing 237 Circular Questions 224 Psychodrama 235
Power in the Family 92	Negotiated Quiet Time 171 Parallel Examples 177 Past Successes 178	Simple Contract 268 Time Cable 270 Problem Solving 264
Projective Identification 93	Caring Days 126 Childhood Home 129 Logical and Natural Consequences 163	Caring Days 243 Childhood Memory 244 Discipline 226, 227
Psychological Distance 94	Family Choreography 146 Family Drawings 148 Video Playback 217	Psychodrama 235 Materials 148 Nonverbal Cues 260
Punctuation 95	Communication Game 132 Looking 164 Unbalancing 214	Communication 225 Nonverbal Cues 260 Journal Format 256
Quid pro Quo 96	Contingency Contract 135 Expectations Game 144 Quid pro Quo 187	Discipline 226, 227 Journal Format 256 Quid pro Quo Cards 265
Reciprocity 97	Communication Game 132 Family Choreography 146 Unbalancing 214	Communication 225 Psychodrama 235 Journal Format 256
Relational Ethics 98	Childhood Home 129 Family Reconstruction 150 Multidirected Partiality 170	Childhood Memory 244 Genogram 231 Journal Format 256
Rituals 99	Fighting Fair 152 Photos 180 Value Assessment 216	Journal Format 256 Childhood Memories 244 Expectations 251
Roles 100	Family Choreography 146 Rejunction 189 Sculpting 196	Psychodrama 235 Foregiveness 254 Psychodrama 235
Rules 101	Rules Identification 194 Rules of Interaction 195 Straightforward Directives 203	Rules 267 Meta-Rules 258 Encouragement 229

continued

THE CONNECTION CHART

PART ONE Concept	PART TWO Techniques	PART THREE Resources
Scapegoating 102	Defining the Problem 138 Marital Schism 165 Triangles 212	Defining the Problem 249 Listening 234 Materials 212
Second-Order Change 103	Positive Double Bind 182 Telegram 206 Touch 209	Journal Format 256 Communication Roadblocks 245 Dimensions of Support 250
Self-Esteem 104	Encouragement 229 Focus on Strength 153 Positive Connotations 181	Encouragement 229 Group Leadership Skills 232 Meta-Rules 258
Shame 105	Childhood Home 129 Defining the Problem 138 Use of Self 215	Childhood Memories 244 Problem Solving 264 Johari Window 255
Sibling Positions 106	Family Choreography 146 Family Drawing 148 Family Reconstruction 150	Psychodrama 235 Materials 148 Genogram 231
Split Loyalties 107	Homework Prescription 158 Triadic Exercises 211 Vulnerability Contract 218	Relabeling 266 Self-Disclosure 238 Vulnerability Contract 272
Strategies 108	Crediting 136 Defining the Problem 138 Rejunction 189	Time Cable 270 Problem Solving 264 Forgiveness Format 254
Subsystems 109	Challenging the Structure 128 Siding 198 Triangles 212	Pathway 263 Dimensions of Support 250 Materials 212
Success Identity 110	Family Council 147 Paradoxical Prescription 176 Positive Reinforcement 183	Family Minutes 252 Anger 242 Discipline 226, 227

Symptom as a
  Metaphor 111
	Awareness
	  Enhancement 122
	Metaphor 167
	Transactional Patterns 210
		Group Leadership
		  Skills 232
		Monitoring 259
		Family Reconstruction 253

THE CONNECTION CHART

PART ONE Concept	PART TWO Techniques	PART THREE Resources
System of Interaction 112	Anatomy of a Relationship 121 Person to Person 179 Video Playback 217	Role Playing 237 Encouragement 229 Nonverbal Cues 260
Target Dimensions 113	Crediting 136 Ordeals 173 Use of Self 215	Time Cable 270 Problem Solving 264 Johari Window 255
Time 114	Detriangling 139 Humor Applied 159 Triadic Exercises 211	Listening 234 Humor 233 Self-Disclosure 238
Time Cable 115	Humor Applied 159 Live History 162 Marital Schism 165	Humor 234 Marriage Model 257 Defining the Problem 249
Triangulation 116	Defining the Problem 138 Psychodrama 186 Triangles 212	Defining the Problem 249 Psychodrama 235 Materials 212
Worldview 117	Behavioral Rehearsal 124 Focus on Strength 153 Self-Disclosure 197	Behavioral Rehearsal 223 Group Leadership Skills 232 Johari Window 255

PART ONE

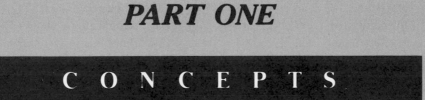

C O N C E P T S

CONCEPT

Accountability

I. Source
Based on Boszormenyi-Nagy, I., with Krasner, B. (1986). *Between give and take: A clinical guide to contextual therapy.* New York: Brunner/Mazel.

II. Brief Description
All actions and interactions have consequences. Regardless of attitudes or excuses, the consequences of a person's actions or interactions, including interpersonal dialogues, are that person's responsibility. Others cannot be blamed for consequences resulting from one's own actions or interactions with others.

III. Initial Statement
Keith, Linda, Anita, and Keith Jr., you are all individuals involved in a family. The family is not responsible for the consequences of your individual actions or interactions. Each of you is accountable for your words and their results. No blame is to be placed on another family member for your actions, attitudes, or interactions. Each of you needs to ask yourself, "What can I say or do to make the situation better?" I hope that each of you learns to choose words carefully, so you communicate your exact feelings and thoughts. This is a step toward taking responsibility for your words, so that healthy communication can develop. Let's try to communicate exactly what we mean, and see the difference when you choose your words carefully.

IV. Follow-Up Techniques
Challenging the communication
Communication game
Multidirected partiality

CONCEPT

Affective Systems

I. Source
Based on Minuchin, S., Montalvo, B., Rosman, B., & Schumer, F. (1967). *Families of the slums.* New York: Basic Books.

II. Brief Description
A family's emotional reaction to an event often reflects the family's affective state rather than the occurrence itself. Because individuals have different emotional reaction patterns, the family's affective system is determined by the composite reactions of all the family members.

III. Initial Statement
Keith and Linda, the situation you are reacting to is more the result of how you feel inside than what is actually happening around you. The anxiety you as a parent experience has more to do with disciplining Anita than her actual behavior. This anxiety can sometimes cause you to lash out at the child closest to you rather than the one who misbehaved. By becoming aware of the feelings that are expressed within the family, we can determine how each member gets in touch with other members. We can learn which feelings are easier, or more acceptable, to express in your family. Learning this will help us work on expressing feelings that are kept hidden but need to come out.

IV. Follow-Up Techniques
Person to person
Ropes
Use of self

CONCEPT

Alignments

I. Source
Based on Boszormenyi-Nagy, I., & Framo, J. (1965). *Intensive family therapy.* New York: Harper & Row.

II. Brief Description
Alignments are the psychological or emotional connections that family members make with one another. Alignments may be positive, when members join together, or negative, when members oppose one another. Each alignment has an impact on the rest of the family.

III. Initial Statement
As I'm watching you all interact, a picture is coming to my mind that I'd like to share with you. You seem to be connected in either supportive or hostile pairs. Keith and Linda, you are very supportive of each other. Kim and Mark are also connected, but in a negative way. Mark, I noticed you criticizing Kim several times tonight. Kim, you seem to be making faces and turning away from Mark. You two are in opposition, and that is your connection.

IV. Follow-Up Techniques
Ropes
Taking sides
Transactional patterns

CONCEPT

Anchoring

I. *Source*
Based on King, M., Novik, L., & Citrenbaum, C. (1983). *Irresistible communication: Creative skills for the health professional.* Philadelphia: W. B. Saunders.

II. *Brief Description*
The concept of anchoring involves the association of particular feelings and thoughts with visual, auditory, and kinesthetic stimuli. If family members are made aware of their automatic reactions to stimuli, they can learn to act rather than always react. (They can also learn to develop and use stimuli to elicit desired reactions from other family members.) Automatic reactions can make it very difficult to change families' patterns of interaction.

III. *Initial Statement*
Linda, did you ever notice how a certain song always puts you in a good mood? I'm noticing something similar, in that your natural reaction when Anita speaks in a certain tone of voice is anger. Always having the same response to a certain kind of sound is a common phenomenon. In order to make healthy change easier, I'd like you to be aware of this phenomenon when it happens. Be aware that Anita's using that tone of voice may not always mean she's discussing something that will make you angry. If you can separate the meaning of her words from the meaning of her tone of voice, you can get a much better understanding of what she is trying to communicate. Although Anita is using the tone that makes you angry, she may be trying to say something new. Once you're aware of your reaction, you can change it. An added benefit of this awareness is that you can learn to push the buttons that make you happy.

IV. *Follow-Up Techniques*
Behavioral rehearsal
Monitoring
Speaker's chair

CONCEPT

Appreciation

I. Source
Based on Deetz, S., & Steven, S. (1986). *Managing interpersonal communication.* New York: Harper & Row.

II. Brief Description
Appreciation is an effort by one person to build another person's self-esteem through acts of love, respect, compliments, and other signs of admiration. The demonstration of heartfelt appreciation is an important skill for family members to learn in order to establish a healthy family.

III. Initial Statement
You've both talked about the things that the other one does or says that irritate you. For example, Linda, you said that Keith does not help with the children enough. Keith, you said that Linda is always cutting you down in front of the children. It sounds as if you are experiencing this family conflict because you are both focusing on negative feelings and actions. Keith, you need to show Linda how much you love her. Linda, you need to show Keith how much you love him. You can build a stronger relationship as husband and wife and as a family by demonstrating love and respect for one another. The children will learn by your example that acts of appreciation are healthy and make everyone happy.

IV. Follow-Up Techniques
Caring days
Crediting
Positive connotations

CONCEPT

Autonomy

I. Source

Based on Gurman, A. (Ed.). (1985). *Casebook of marital therapy.* New York: Guilford Press.

II. Brief Description

Autonomy is the capacity for independent survival. Independent thinking and judgment and intrinsic self-approval are characteristics of the autonomous personality. Autonomous individuals look for approval within themselves rather than in the social environment. The ultimate goal of parenting is to raise autonomous, independent children.

III. Initial Statement

Linda and Keith, sometimes we as individuals become so caught up in our family life and its interpersonal demands and emotional traffic that we lose sight of ourselves. We almost become fused together, as engine parts do when they overheat and melt. If this happens in a family, its members can lose some or even all of their sense of self as individuals. One job of the family is to help children develop their individual selves. But just like those engine parts, we as individual family members can fuse together under stress. When this happens, we stop functioning effectively as individuals and as a family.

IV. Follow-Up Techniques

"I" statements
Prescribing the symptom
Value assessment

CONCEPT

Behavioral Change

I. Source
Based on Corey, G. (1991). *Theory and practice of counseling and psychotherapy* (4th ed.). Pacific Grove, CA: Brooks/Cole.

II. Brief Description
The process of behavioral change has three phases. First, in self-observation, clients observe their own behavior and what it tells them about themselves. Second, by starting a new internal dialogue, clients begin to choose alternative patterns that lead to behavioral, cognitive, and affective change. And finally, by learning new skills and practicing them in real-life situations, clients find that as they behave differently, they typically get different reactions from others.

III. Initial Statement
Linda, I hear you say that you will never make it through this family transition period because you always fail at anything you try. Let's listen to what you are telling yourself. Is that what you really want to believe? What would you like to tell yourself? Once you start to tell yourself these positive things, you will notice that your behavior changes to match your thoughts. The people around you will respond to you in a different, more positive way. You will find you can develop new ways for dealing with family problems and have the courage to try them!

IV. Follow-Up Techniques
Behavioral rehearsal
Reverse role playing
Role playing

CONCEPT

Behavioral Rehearsal

I. *Source*
Based on Thompson, C., & Rudolph, L. (1992). *Counseling children* (3rd ed.). Pacific Grove, CA: Brooks/Cole.

II. *Brief Description*
Behavioral rehearsal involves practicing a new behavior in the safe environment of a counseling session before actually attempting the behavior in the real world. This practice allows a person or a whole family to obtain feedback and develop confidence while practicing the behavior. Behavioral rehearsal also allows the rest of the family to see how an individual is trying to change.

III. *Initial Statement*
Linda and Anita, I've noticed that when you try to communicate with each other, sarcasm and yelling tends to dominate the conversation. I would like to see the two of you effectively communicate by patiently listening to each other, speaking in calm voices, and responding only after the other has finished speaking. For the next ten minutes, I want the two of you to have a conversation practicing these rules. This means you will have to try something new, which is scary but will help both of you in the future.

IV. *Follow-Up Techniques*
Behavioral rehearsal
Challenging the communication
Telegram

CONCEPT

Benevolent Sabotage

I. Source
Based on Watzlawick, P., Weakland, J. H., & Fisch, R. (1974). *Change: Principles of problem formation and problem resolution.* New York: W. W. Norton.

II. Brief Description
Benevolent sabotage is a reframing technique typically used in families with a juvenile delinquent whose parents are overtly harsh and domineering but covertly permissive. With this technique, the parents' attitude toward the child changes to one of benevolence. They respond to the child's behavior with passive aggression, depriving the child of reasons to rebel against harsh parental control.

III. Initial Statement
Keith and Linda, I think the rules of the game have changed in your family. You are finding out that the kinds of things you may have used to guide and control your son when he was, say, eight years old no longer work now that he is fourteen. So this is what I want you to do: When Keith Jr. misbehaves you are to act dumb but loving. For instance, if he gets home late, lock the door—sort of accidentally—so he can't get in for a while. Then say, "Gee, we're sorry. We thought everyone was already in for the night." This may be a better way to teach him to be on time than what you have been doing up until now. I know that this approach may strike you, as caring parents, as a harsh and punitive tactic, but it is really a loving way to teach him that his behavior has natural consequences. He will probably act really angry at you for a while. Stick it out, and remember, it's the behavior you're targeting, not the child.

IV. Follow-Up Techniques
Paradoxical double bind
Reframing
Rules of interaction

CONCEPT

Birth Order

I. *Source*
Based on Toman, W. (1961). *Family constellations: A psychological game.* New York: Springer.

II. *Brief Description*
Birth order, simply stated, describes the ordinal position children hold within a family. Social scientists have long believed that whether you are an only child, the oldest, in the middle, or the youngest has a great deal to do with the development of your personality. As each child joins the family, changes occur that impact those already in the family. The number of years between children also affects how children perceive themselves.

III. *Initial Statement*
Apart from individual personalities, there could be some very good reasons people in this family act the way they do. Oldest children—like you, Keith Jr.—are often very responsible and intense. They can be the ones who start fights or the ones who see both sides of the conflict. Middle children, like Kim and Mark, often feel picked on or unimportant. They're also good at using guilt trips to get what they want. Ruth, being the youngest, is treated like other youngest children: everyone helps her, but at the same time she's treated as a tagalong. Youngest children are often dramatic and manipulative in order to get the attention they crave. We can look at how birth order affects the way you act in your family. We can also talk about how birth orders have changed since your family has been blended.

IV. *Follow-Up Techniques*
Childhood home
Marital stalemate
Sociogram

CONCEPT

Boundaries

I. Source
Based on Rosenblatt, P. C. (1994). *Metaphors of family systems theory.* New York: Guilford Press.

II. Brief Description
A boundary is an invisible line that separates a system, subsystem, or individual from outside surroundings. Boundaries must be sufficiently well defined to allow subsystem members to carry out tasks and still be open enough to permit contact between members of subsystems and others. In this way the autonomy of the subsystem is protected while the interdependence of all the family's subsystems is maintained.

III. Initial Statement
Linda and Keith, from what you have said, the level of tension between the two of you increases when Linda's mother comes for a visit and starts to parent your children and reorganize your home. The important thing to remember is that these are your children and this is your home. You are creating a family with its own roles, rules, and responsibilities. Linda, your mother has to respect the line between herself and your immediate family. It is possible for your mother to be closely involved with your family, but she must respect the fact that it is your family. If she tries to act like a parent or change family rules, she will confuse your children and frustrate what you and Keith are trying to accomplish.

IV. Follow-Up Techniques
Enactment
Genogram
Taking sides

CONCEPT

Calibration

I. Source
Based on Piercy, F., Sprenkle, D., et al. (1986). *Family therapy sourcebook*. New York: Guilford Press.

II. Brief Description
The identification of rules that exist in the family system and the attempt to adjust behavior to fit them are what is called calibration. Covert and overt rules are developed using feedback from family members. Calibration can work both positively and negatively. Family members gauge the appropriateness of their actions by the reactions of the other members.

III. Initial Statement
Every family has its own rules about the way members interact. Your family has created rules of interacting that one or more of you may want to change. In order to change the rules, you must first identify them. You learn to redefine these rules according to the feedback or feelings each member has about the rules. Linda and Anita, it seems to me that you have a rule that you have to be angry with each other so that you will not get close. If you do get close to each other, and this family breaks up, you will have to go through the same pain you went through when your other family broke up.

IV. Follow-Up Techniques
Restructuring
Rules identification
Rules of interaction

CONCEPT

Chemical Dependency

I. Source
Based on Cleveland, M. (1981). "Families and Adolescent Drug Abuse: Structural Analysis of Children's Roles." *Family Process*, 20.

II. Brief Description
There are many roles within a chemically dependent family. Family members react to a chemical dependency within the family by assuming different functions. Each role is characterized by different behaviors and feelings. Typical roles have been identified as chief enabler, hero, scapegoat, caregiver, and adjuster. Each role contributes to how the family is functioning.

III. Initial Statement
Keith, the alcoholism in your family has affected all of you. Each of you has reacted to the alcoholism in your own way, and as a result each of you has assumed a role that serves a unique purpose. We need to identify your individual roles and what purpose they have been serving. (An explanation of the roles typical of chemically dependent families can be provided at this point.) Can you recognize yourself in any of these roles?

IV. Follow-Up Techniques
Challenging the structure
Conflict management
Transactional patterns

CONCEPT

Circular Causality

I. Source
Based on Wynne, L., McDaniel, S., & Weber, T. (1986). *Systems consultation: A new perspective for family therapy.* New York: Guilford Press.

II. Brief Description
Interactions among family members produce a cycle of behavioral responses. Each person involved in an interaction influences and has been influenced by another person's behavior. These influences can be both positive and negative, and they tend to reinforce the behavior of other family members, perpetuating the cycle of responses.

III. Initial Statement
If I hear you correctly, Keith, you feel that Linda's constant complaining causes you to spend less and less time at home. Linda, you feel that it is Keith's frequent absences that cause you to complain a lot when he is around. I would like to suggest that neither one of you is completely at fault or completely innocent in this situation. Keith, maybe Linda's complaining does push you away, but your frequent absences from home only give Linda more to complain about. Linda, maybe Keith does give you lots to complain about, but by focusing only on your complaints, you push him away even further. Each of you, by acting the way you do, encourages the very behavior that you say you don't like in the other person. Rather than focusing on who started this cycle, why don't we work to figure out how to break out of it?

IV. Follow-Up Techniques
Circular questions
Defining the problem
Role playing

CONCEPT

Circularity

I. Source

Based on Hoffman, L. (1981). *Foundations of family therapy.* New York: Basic Books.

II. Brief Description

Circularity is a process of interaction among members of a family system or subsystem in which each member's behavior is simultaneously caused by and causative of behavior in another part of the system. Causality of a problem is not viewed as the interaction of stimulus and effect, but rather as occurring within the context of relationships. Therefore, the problem does not reside within one person. The person's behavior must be seen in a context in which another person is present who exchanges information. Each influences the other. The focus is on information.

III. Initial Statement

I want you to picture a fish pond in which one fish jumps up to snap at a bug. That fish's jumping starts other fish jumping, creating more waves on the pond, which stir up more bugs, which cause more fish to jump. Your family is like the fish in a pond. You are all in the pond together and you seem to feed off one another's behavior. For example, Keith is having financial difficulty. He yells at Linda for keeping too many lights on in the house and running up the electric bill. Linda in turn tries to save money by refusing to give Keith Jr. gas money for his car. He gets resentful and begins to break curfew. Keith Sr. punishes his son, making him even more resentful and causing him to threaten to move out and live with a friend.

IV. Follow-Up Techniques

Monitoring
Pretend
Self-disclosure

CONCEPT

Closed System

I. *Source*
Based on Brown, J., & Christensen, D. (1986). *Family Therapy: Theory and practice.* Pacific Grove, CA: Brooks/Cole.

II. *Brief Description*
A family characterized by restricted communication among family members because of fear of retaliation has what is called a closed family system. Family members often subordinate their needs for the benefit of the group. Indications of a closed system include rigidity, suspiciousness, sarcasm, recklessness, and isolation. A family with a closed system tends to be closed to outsiders and is much more likely to become dysfunctional.

III. *Initial Statement*
Keith and Linda, sometimes a family can close itself off from the rest of the world and become isolated. Though excluding some outside people and influences can be beneficial to the family or its individual members, shutting out everyone can be destructive. A good analogy is a lake: if the streams feeding it dry up, and it has little or no drainage, the lake will become stagnant. A family needs to interact with others in order to keep itself healthy and fresh.

IV. *Follow-Up Techniques*
Self-disclosure
Storytelling
Transactional patterns

CONCEPT

Coevolution

I. Source
Based on Bateson, G. (1979). *Mind and nature: A necessary unity.* New York: E. P. Dutton.

II. Brief Description
Coevolution is a way of describing how change takes place within the family system. According to this concept, each member impacts or affects the development and growth of every other member of the family. Within the context of therapy session, the therapist is also viewed as a member of the family system, who will impact change and growth. The change that takes place can be either positive or negative.

III. Initial Statement
Let's look at how change occurs in your family and how each family interaction affects others in your family. Linda, you have expressed frustration with Anita when she ignores you. You do not challenge Anita directly, and so Anita continues the negative behavior. You then complain to Keith about his daughter's behavior and ask him to address it with her. Keith, you are hesitant to talk with Anita because you don't witness the behavior firsthand. Linda, you now feel frustrated with Keith as well as with Anita. As a result of Keith's reaction to your concern, you have decided to confront Anita directly. This example shows how interactions within one set of family members, Linda and Anita, impact interactions within a second set, Linda and Keith, causing a change in future interactions between Linda and Anita.

IV. Follow-Up Techniques
Boundaries
Circular interview
Joining

CONCEPT

Communication Styles

I. *Source*
Based on Satir, V. (1972). *Peoplemaking.* Palo Alto, CA: Science and Behavior Books.

II. *Brief Description*
Virginia Satir identified five styles of communication that occur between individuals when one of them is under stress. These styles are as follows: The placater always agrees, tries to please, and apologizes. The blamer dominates, accuses, and finds fault. The super-reasonable person is detached, cool, calm, and not emotionally involved. The irrelevant person distracts others and seems unable to relate to what's going on. The communicator seems real and genuinely expressive, and sends straight messages. Satir believes that all of these styles except that of the communicator prevent people from exposing their true feelings.

III. *Initial Statement*
Linda and Keith, when family members experience stress they begin to relate to other family members in one of five ways. These five ways are those of the blamer, the placater, the communicator, the super-reasonable person, and the irrelevant person. Your family is also using these styles of communication. Let's talk about some of the styles that your family is using and the impact those styles are having on you individually.

IV. *Follow-Up Techniques*
Communication stances
Looking
Photos

CONCEPT

Complementary Relationship

I. *Source*

Based on Hurvitz, N., & Straus, R. (1991). *Marriage and family therapy: A sociocognitive approach.* New York: Haworth Press.

II. *Brief Description*

A complementary relationship is a pattern of interaction characterized by inequality and maximization of differences between two people. A good example is a relationship in which one person is dominant and the other is submissive. Each person behaves in a manner that presupposes and at the same time provides a rationale for the behavior of the other.

III. *Initial Statement*

Keith, I can see in your interaction with Linda that you assume a one-down position, which puts Linda in a one-up position. You say you are depressed, but it is your inaction that encourages Linda to make all the decisions and have all the say. Linda's active role in turn makes you less active. I think both of you would agree that neither is benefiting from this relationship. Now, let's see what we can do about changing your pattern of interaction.

IV. *Follow-Up Techniques*

Paradoxical double bind
Rules of interaction
Taking sides

CONCEPT

Compliment

I. *Source*
Based on de Shazer, S. (1992). *Patterns of brief family therapy: An ecosystemic approach.* New York: Guilford Press.

II. *Brief Description*
A compliment is a positive statement delivered by the therapist about a family or family member in terms that are consistent with the family's communication style. The family is more likely to agree with a statement delivered this way, and that agreement facilitates the family's acceptance of the intervention that follows. The compliment reframes the issue; it must be true, or the family will feel manipulated.

III. *Initial Statement*
You've each described the problem and that has been helpful. I can see that you all care for your father and want very much to help him past his withdrawal problems. I've also noticed that you care so much that any one of you would do just about anything to help him from facing the consequences of his withdrawal. Most other families would not try to protect him. You've shown your loyalty. Now let's talk about what your father needs to do for himself.

IV. *Follow-Up Techniques*
Communication game
Encouraging
Restructuring

CONCEPT

Cooperating

I. *Source*
Based on Dinkmeyer, D., & Carlson, J. (1984). *Time for a better marriage.* Circle Pines, MN: American Guidance Services.

II. *Brief Description*
Being a member of a family is like being a member of a team. As members, we all behave in ways that respond to the patterns of our team. This behavior is cooperating. When some members do not cooperate, others must accommodate them or change their assignments. Often, a family member verbally agrees to start cooperating, but does not change his or her behavior.

III. *Initial Statement*
In your family, you have a specific pattern you follow to get everyone out the door to work and school in the morning. Kim makes lunches, Keith drops Ruth at the sitter's, and Anita is supposed to do the breakfast dishes, although you have all said that she often skips this job. You are asking everyone in the family to work as a team. Anita's response to this request is to not do her part. Only some of your morning tasks are completed, and either the house is left messy or someone is late to school or work.

IV. *Follow-Up Techniques*
Conflict management
Family reconstruction
Harmony among parts

CONCEPT

Coping Ability

I. *Source*
Based on Bedrosian, R., & Bozicas, G. D. (1994). *Treating family of origin problems: A cognitive approach.* New York: Guilford Press.

II. *Brief Description*
Coping ability involves adjusting, adapting, and successfully dealing with a challenge. A family's coping ability depends on its health as a family. A healthy family copes with a crisis through family strength and individual growth. Immediate and extended family members pull together to aid one another during the crisis. A crisis tends to tear apart an unhealthy family, making coping more difficult. One way that an unhealthy family copes is by blaming other members for the crisis and not responding at all.

III. *Initial Statement*
Sometimes, unexpected situations occur that really test a family. Each family handles these tests in a different way. The strengths and weaknesses of a family come out during a crisis. As I see it, in your family, bonds were broken by divorce; this new family needs time to grow together. That time has been cut short because Anita's issues have put you into a crisis phase. Your family's ability to cope will depend on us working together to find the positive aspects of your family life and work out the negative ones. It is important for all of you to pull together and allow the family to grow stronger.

IV. *Follow-Up Techniques*
Harmony among parts
Prescribing the symptom
Tickling of defenses

CONCEPT

Cybernetics

I. *Source*
Based on Bateson, G. (1972). *Steps to an ecology of mind.* New York: Ballantine Books.

II. *Brief Description*
When the family system becomes involved in therapy, the therapist becomes a part of a coevolving ecosystem. The therapist and the family affect each other in circular feedback loops, which means that interactions can be directed toward the therapist as well as the family members. The therapist is not considered neutral, but part of the therapeutic communication with the family.

III. *Initial Statement*
Keith and Linda, you need to understand that all of us are involved in interacting while we are together. As a therapist, I am part of your interactions and am actively involved in the changes occurring in your family. All of us in these sessions influence one another and are therefore involved in the process. Understanding my involvement should help define my role and actions as we continue in therapy. I will ask questions and expect responses from you. I consider it good for you to ask me questions, and I will give you feedback. We are in the process of becoming a healthier family unit.

IV. *Follow-Up Techniques*
Family drawings
Parallel examples
Role playing

CONCEPT

Delegation

I. *Source*

Stierlin, H. (1974). *Separating parents and adolescents.* New York: Quadrangle/New York Times Book Company.

II. *Brief Description*

In some families, children are often unconsciously chosen by their parents or grandparents to fulfill a certain mission. A child is "delegated" a particular role and in return for fulfilling it gains self-esteem. When a couple is having difficulty, one child may be delegated the role of scapegoat to alleviate the pressure within the couple. The child is given credit for performing this function for the family.

III. *Initial Statement*

Keith and Linda, I've heard a lot about conflicts between Kim and Mark and between Linda and Anita. I'm wondering how Ruth is doing. Because she is the child of your marriage, I wonder whether she's been delegated the role of "good kid": as long as she is good and doesn't cause any problems amidst this chaos, you two, her parents, will stay together. If this is true, have you thought about what roles you have unconsciously assigned to your other children?

IV. *Follow-Up Techniques*

Crediting
Multidirected partiality
Straightforward directives

CONCEPT

Developmental Tasks

I. Source

Based on Barker, P. (1981). *Basic family therapy.* Baltimore, MD: University Park Press.

II. Brief Description

Each family has developmental phases that take place throughout the family life cycle. Each phase presents the family with particular tasks to be achieved. These developmental tasks revolve around change in the family's structure or situation. During this time, family rules may need to be changed or modified. Most problems are created and intensified when the family is presented with new issues but cannot modify its rules.

III. Initial Statement

Keith and Linda, integrating your children and yourselves together into a family is a big job. Each family member will need to do some adjusting for this family to move forward. Linda and Keith, you both need to see how you can help your children to move on for the benefit of the family. The first step in this process is for us to get a clear picture of how all seven of you see your current living arrangements.

IV. Follow-Up Techniques

Circular questions
Parallel examples
Time out

CONCEPT

Differentiation of Self

I. Source
Based on Bowen, M. (1974). Toward the differentiation of self in one's own family of origin. In P. Lorio & F. Andres (Eds.), *Georgetown family symposia* (Vol. I). Washington, DC: Department of Psychiatry, Georgetown Medical Center.

II. Brief Description
Differentiation is the ability to resist being overwhelmed by another person's emotional reactions through the ability to separate your thoughts from those feelings. Differentiated people are in touch with their feelings and think of what is best for themselves rather than acceding to others' desires or attempts at control. People tend to select mates who have achieved the same level of differentiation as they themselves have. The goal is to achieve a level of differentiation that allows the individual to act and think independently.

III. Initial Statement
Linda and Keith, to be your own person means that you have the ability to be in touch with your own feelings and thoughts and to think of what is best for yourself rather than doing whatever will keep the peace or win someone else's approval. A person with a strong sense of self does not compromise that self to achieve harmony or run away from a situation to avoid taking a stand. We tend to choose partners whose sense of self is as healthy as our own. Your biggest job now is to help your children become strong and ultimately independent of you, so that their chances of a healthy relationship in the future are increased.

IV. Follow-Up Techniques
Looking
Telegram
Unbalancing

CONCEPT

Discontinuous Change

I. Source
Based on Hoffman, L. (1988). The family life cycle and discontinuous change. In B. Carter & M. McGoldrick (Eds.), *The changing family life cycles: A framework for family therapy* (2nd ed.). New York: Gardner Press.

II. Brief Description
In the family life cycle, periods of transition, particularly those marked by members entering or exiting the family, produce great stress. Some families are able to negotiate these transitions smoothly. In others, the resistance to change intensifies as the pressure to change increases. This blocking response, an attempt to maintain homeostasis, can result in symptom formation. When the pressure to change finally builds to the point of overwhelming the family's attempt to block it, one result is that the family becomes able to make the leap to a new level of functioning.

III. Initial Statement
Linda, the members of your family, separately and together, are going through one of life's difficult transitions. It is a major task, especially in the context of a newly formed family. Give yourselves a little leeway to acknowledge and express how stressful this transition is. Your family has been adjusting for six years now and the pressure has increased tremendously. By confronting these challenges rather than ignoring them, your family will end up learning new ways of solving problems and will get stronger and healthier.

IV. Follow-Up Techniques
Negotiation
Paradoxical interventions
Skeleton keys

CONCEPT

Discrimination of Differences

I. *Source*

Based on Bateson, G. (1972). *Steps to an ecology of mind.* New York: Ballantine Books.

II. *Brief Description*

Discrimination of differences is a way of helping families see in what ways events differ from one another. This perspective allows people to think about the differences in one another's perspectives nonjudgmentally and to compare the present situation with what might happen in the future.

III. *Initial Statement*

Each of you has a different way of seeing what's going on between Linda and Anita, and none of you is right or wrong. Because each of you has your own relationships with Linda and Anita, your view is influenced by what you see and know. It may help us to get a more complete picture of what's going on if we hear from each of you how you see the situation now and how you think it might look in the future. Then we may understand Linda and Anita's difficulties more fully.

IV. *Follow-Up Techniques*

Circular questions
Defining the problem
Marital schism

CONCEPT

Disengagement

I. Source
Based on Minuchin, S. (1974). *Families and family therapy.* Cambridge, MA: Harvard University Press.

II. Brief Description
Disengagement refers to a style of family interaction in which members are isolated and disconnected from one another, with each member functioning separately and autonomously. Positively, disengagement can lead to independence and self-reliance; negatively, it can limit needed affection, support, and guidance. Disengagement often occurs in blended families, and it tends to be generalized to other relationships.

III. Initial Statement
Mr. Evans, I am the school counselor; I asked you to come here today because your daughter is failing two of her subjects. Anita has been absent too many days this year and has been picked up by the police for truancy and shoplifting. I understand that you are currently involved in family counseling. This is a good first step, but I do feel that you have become cut off from Anita, and she misses your involvement in her life. Anita needs your support to get through the difficult teenage years. I see your increased involvement as the key to helping her.

IV. Follow-Up Techniques
Homework prescriptions
Triangles
Value assessment

CONCEPT

Displacement

I. *Source*
Based on Guerin, P. J. (1971). A family affair. In P. Lorio & F. Andres (Eds.), *Georgetown Family Symposia* (Vol. I). Washington, DC: Department of Psychiatry, Georgetown Medical Center.

II. *Brief Description*
Displacement is the unconscious redirection of energy, such as anger, from one person or object to a substitute that is less threatening or more readily available. Children often observe and copy unconscious process.

III. *Initial Statement*
Linda, you said earlier that part of your frustration with Keith is that he comes home from work in a bad mood and takes everything out on you. It sounds to me like you think this treatment is unfair. I suspect, Keith, that you are unaware of how your behavior makes Linda feel. You may even be unaware that you are taking out on her the anger you feel toward your boss. I want to help you both work on learning to cope better with outside frustrations and to be more sensitive toward each other.

IV. *Follow-Up Techniques*
Empty chair
Person to person
Marital stalemate

CONCEPT

Distance Regulation

I. *Source*

Based on Kantor, D., & Lehr, W. (1975). *Inside the family.* San Francisco: Jossey-Bass.

II. *Brief Description*

One goal within families and their subsystems is to maintain a proper distance, or degree of interpersonal closeness, for each family member. This interpersonal distance is monitored and maintained through patterns of interaction and roles within the family. Each individual family member helps determine and regulate the proper distance. Conflict occurs when these distances are violated.

III. *Initial Statement*

Keith and Linda, you've heard people say things like "You're in my space" or "I need more space." Each of you has your own comfort level when it comes to emotional space. Keith, you've said you're a pretty private person and that in your first marriage your wife left you alone most of the time. Linda, you, on the other hand, have told us how important it is for you to have a close relationship with your husband. It looks as though one reason for your arguments is that each of you is trying to put the other at a comfortable emotional distance. It would be a good idea for the family to talk about their needs for space and closeness and to work out a way for each member to feel comfortable.

IV. *Follow-Up Techniques*

Ropes
Sculpting
Vulnerability contract

CONCEPT

Distractor Role

I. *Source*
Based on Thompson, C. L., & Rudolph, L. B. (1992). *Counseling children.* Pacific Grove, CA: Brooks/Cole.

II. *Brief Description*
The distractor role is one of the universal response roles a person may take in communicating with others. It is used to hide real feelings out of fear of rejection. The distractor changes the subject so as not to deal with the issues at hand. Both parents and children use this role to avoid dealing with issues.

III. *Initial Statement*
Keith Jr., I've noticed that when our discussion focuses on you, you tend to change the subject and evade the issue. Some of the things you say are really off the wall. For example, when Linda said you would rather watch baseball than go miniature golfing with your family, you said, "Baseball is my life. I know who will be the next National League's MVP." It's as if you believe that if you change the subject often enough, maybe the problem will go away. Ignoring the issue allows you to hide your real feelings but does nothing to solve the problem.

IV. *Follow-Up Techniques*
Communication game
Positive reinforcement
Video playback

CONCEPT

Double Bind

I. *Source*

Based on Bateson, G., Jackson, D., Haley, J., & Weakland, J. (1956). Toward a theory of schizophrenia. *Behavioral Science, 1,* 251–264.

II. *Brief Description*

A double bind involves two people who are in an important, ongoing relationship. The first person gives a primary negative message, which is followed by an inconsistent and conflicting second message. Both messages are enforced by a third message of punishment or perceived threat, meaning that a response or behavior is demanded. The person receiving these messages becomes confused and feels victimized.

III. *Initial Statement*

Keith and Linda, all of us from time to time experience the feeling that "we're damned if we do and damned if we don't." You may feel angry or frustrated because you feel that no matter what you do, you can't win. This situation can come about when a person sends out loving messages to another, but withdraws or becomes hostile when the second person comes too close. In a marriage, for example, a wife may encourage her husband, only to reject him when he comes too close. With a child, the parent may send out loving messages, but when the child comes too close physically or emotionally, the child is clearly told to go away. Has your family ever played this game?

IV. *Follow-Up Techniques*

Enactment
Telegram
Worst alternative

CONCEPT

Emotional Cutoff

I. Source
Based on Gurman, A. S., & Kniskern, D. P. (Eds.). (1981). *Handbook of family therapy*. New York: Brunner/Mazel.

II. Brief Description
Emotional cutoff describes a common way people deal with unresolved conflicts and fusion in their families of origin: by emotionally distancing or insulating themselves from family members. This cutoff may be accomplished by maintaining a geographic separation, by limiting family contacts to the brief and superficial, or by employing psychological mechanisms such as avoidance, withdrawal, and denial while in the company of family.

III. Initial Statement
Keith, I'd like you to think about any similarities you might see between what you described as a distant relationship with your parents when you were a teenager and your concern about Keith Jr.'s rebelliousness and withdrawal from the family now. What I see happening here is history repeating itself. I see Keith Jr. reacting to you and the family in much the same way as you emotionally escaped from your own parents' overprotectiveness. I see Keith Jr. responding to the family in a similar way when he goes to his room or leaves the house whenever there are arguments, threatens to run away, or refuses to go anywhere or do anything with the family. Keith Jr., what happens at home that makes you feel scared and want to get away from everyone?

IV. Follow-Up Techniques
Fighting fair
Looking
Rules of interaction

CONCEPT

Enabling Family

I. *Source*

Based on Kantor, D., & Lehr, W. (1975). *Inside the family.* San Francisco: Jossey-Bass.

II. *Brief Description*

The various parts or subsystems of a family each have their own goals. Competition and conflict are bound to arise as these different goals are pursued. An enabling family is able to maintain closeness among members and subsystems without denying the possibility of obtaining the goals being sought on a regular basis by any one member or subsystem. Although any one person's goals may be temporarily sacrificed from time to time, family members are still able to cooperate with one another.

III. *Initial Statement*

You each have your own goals within your family. Linda, your goal is to feel constant affection and comfort with Keith. Keith attempts to help you achieve this goal by reacting to your needs for warmth. But Anita wants Keith's affection too, and she feels threatened by you, Linda. She creates a conflict with you, which creates stress between you and Keith. In an ideal situation, each of you would have an opportunity to achieve your individual goals, while the others are also enabled to reach their goals. What we can work on here is helping you work together so that you can all get what you want by helping the others get what they want. Linda, you can reassure Anita that you won't take away her father's love for her. Keith, you can do the same for Anita and Linda by easing the conflict between them, reassuring each of them of your affection.

IV. *Follow-Up Techniques*

Family council
Skeleton keys
Marital stalemate

CONCEPT

Enmeshment

I. Source
Based on Minuchin, S., & Fishman, H. C. (1981). *Family therapy techniques.* Cambridge, MA: Harvard University Press.

II. Brief Description
Enmeshment is an extreme form of closeness and intensity in family interactions, with members overly concerned and involved in one another's lives. The family's lack of differentiation makes any separation from the family an act of betrayal. Belonging to the family and protecting the family secret dominates all experiences at the expense of each member's developing a separate sense of self. In an enmeshed family, subsystem boundaries are poorly differentiated.

III. Initial Statement
It seems to me that each of you is overly concerned about how someone else feels. You, Keith, are feeling responsible for Linda's feelings. Linda, you are reacting to Keith's feelings of guilt. The children feel they're the cause of Keith's withdrawal, Keith in turn worries more, so he withdraws further. The cycle keeps repeating itself, and everyone is owning everyone else's feelings. In reality, each of us is responsible for our own set of feelings, and all these feelings are OK. The problem is in determining what belongs to each of us. When we identify and claim what we are responsible for, we can change. In a healthy family, the members have a sense of "I-ness." They have an understanding that might be expressed as follows: "I am me. You are you. This is where I end and you begin. I am not responsible for your happiness or sadness, nor are you responsible for mine. None of us is that powerful." Keith's withdrawal in response to family stress has been his choice, selected from the options he knew about to deal with his feelings. Linda, you and the children did not cause the withdrawal, you can't cure it, and you can't control it. Withdrawal is Keith's choice. You have your own separate issues as a result of this family problem. Those are the issues that you and the children need to address.

IV. Follow-Up Techniques
Boundaries
"I" statements
Sociogram

CONCEPT

Entitlement

I. Source
Based on Boszormenyi-Nagy, I., & Krasner, B. R. (1986). *Between give and take: A clinical guide to contextual therapy.* New York: Brunner/Mazel.

II. Brief Description
The person who displays care and concern earns merit or entitlement as a reward. Parenting is a relationship that engenders entitlement. The entitlement that is earned results in benefits for both the caregiver and the receiver. For example, in adequate parenting, the child receives due care while the parent experiences a sense of joy, an expanded sense of self, and an increased functional capacity.

III. Initial Statement
Keith, I know that while your father has been mentally ill, you have stuck by him. I think this is one way you feel you can repay him for raising you. But your father's insistence that you return his care in equal measure is, I feel, a destructive demand. Your father's demand is a result of his illness. Parenting is a debt that can never be repaid. Of course your father needs your care and concern, and I know he deserves it, but the only way you can repay him for his efforts as a parent is to care for your children the way he cared for you.

IV. Follow-Up Techniques
Formula task
Motivation
Past successes

CONCEPT

Exoneration

I. Source
Based on Boszormenyi-Nagy, I., & Krasner, B. R. (1986). *Between give and take: A clinical guide to contextual therapy.* New York: Brunner/Mazel.

II. Brief Description
Exoneration is a process of reassessing another's actions. Someone you may have in the past considered blameworthy you now through new understanding consider blameless. Each person carries issues from childhood or past experiences, which the therapist can help resolve. The child or adult offspring forgives parents for past abuse, emotional, physical, or sexual. The child or adult offspring must come to terms with that hurt and forgive parents in order to be free to love others.

III. Initial Statement
Keith, you now have a deep appreciation for your parents' efforts and limitations, and you see them in a new light. You may not have forgiven them, but you have begun to understand the reasons behind some of their actions. Keith and Linda, sometimes parents can be deliberately cruel to their children for reasons unknown to the child or to anyone else. Surviving abuse and emerging from a dysfunctional family is a great accomplishment and something you should be proud of. You made it through very tough times and became very successful in your careers. However, Keith, you have expressed concern over your inability to have an intimate relationship with your son. In my opinion, what is holding you back is your anger, fear, and resentment surrounding your childhood abuse. You need to acknowledge these feelings and get them out in the open so that we can deal with them. Our goal is ultimately for you to experience forgiveness toward your parents.

IV. Follow-Up Techniques
Childhood home
Family secrets
Formula task

CONCEPT

Family Life Cycle

I. Source
Based on Haley, J. (1973). *Uncommon therapy: The psychiatric techniques of Milton H. Erickson, M.D.* New York: Norton.

II. Brief Description
The family life cycle consists of various stages of development beginning with the partners' marriage and the birth of their first child, through the partners' death or permanent separation. If a crisis or disruption has been unsuccessfully resolved, it will resurface and cause difficulty when the family attempts to move on to the next stage of development. Often, the onset of psychiatric symptoms in a family member coincides with the stage in the life cycle where the family left a crisis unresolved. However, if the family has developed some resources along the way, these can be used to promote growth and change.

III. Initial Statement
Families pass through various stages of development beginning with marriage of the partners. When there is a crisis, the family is prevented from moving smoothly onto the next stage of development. As a result, one person in the family may develop a serious problem that causes the whole family to get stuck in a particular stage of development. I'd like to know exactly what was going on in each of your lives when Keith and Linda first decided to get married. I'd also like you to try to remember whether anything unusual or upsetting happened in the family just before the wedding. Now, I'd also like to know how you've coped with the problems, because that will be a clue to how you can help yourselves to adjust to current and future family changes.

IV. Follow-Up Techniques
Encouraging
Genogram
Typical day

CONCEPT

Family Myths

I. *Source*
Based on McGoldrick, M., Pearce, J. K., & Giordano, J. (1982). *Ethnicity and family therapy.* New York: Guilford Press.

II. *Brief Description*
A family myth is a way that a family presents a lifestyle that follows prescribed norms, even if family members' actual behavior does not. For example, a wife may say that her husband is the boss, although the therapist and the rest of the family are all aware that she is dominating the therapy session and the family. If cultural norms also support the incongruency, it can also be labeled a cultural myth.

III. *Initial Statement*
Keith, as head of the family, I understand your desire to make change in the family that will ease your present situation. With your permission, I will ask your wife, Linda, to help you by reminding you of ways of child rearing— ways you know about, but that Linda may be able to articulate more easily because she carries them out more often, while you are busy with other important business and household matters.

IV. *Follow-Up Techniques*
Family secrets
Homework prescriptions
Reframing

CONCEPT

Family Pet

I. *Source*
Based on Boszormenyi-Nagy, I., & Spark, G. M. (1973). *Invisible loyalties: Reciprocity in intergenerational family therapy.* New York: Harper & Row.

II. *Brief Description*
The family pet is the child, often the youngest, who brings lightness and laughter into the family. This child causes no real problems, is often seen as a good student, may be humorous, and is favorably compared to other siblings for being "good" and undemanding. Despite outward appearances, the family pet is often sad, depressed, and empty inside. Since families tend to overlook the emotions of children in this situation, they may suffer from low self-esteem and feel as though they have no place in their families.

III. *Initial Statement*
Keith and Linda, Anita's concerns seem to be taking up a lot of your attention. It's easy for parents to get bogged down with the problems of a child who is rebelling or causing worry. And then it's all too easy to ignore or forget about the needs of the quiet, more obedient child. I haven't seen you help Ruth to know how special she is as a member of your family. I believe that Ruth must feel she is valuable and has a special place in the family. I would like you all to think about what Ruth might be feeling as you've glossed over her needs in giving Anita's needs more attention.

IV. *Follow-Up Techniques*
Encouraging
Monitoring
Triangles

CONCEPT

Family Structure

I. Source
Based on Minuchin, S. (1974). *Families and family therapy.* Cambridge, MA: Harvard University Press.

II. Brief Description
Family structure is the invisible set of demands, codes, and rules that organize the ways family members interact in order to fulfill family functions. Family structure consists of the transactional patterns that operate in the family. Repeated interactions among family members establish patterns that govern how, when, and with whom individuals interact, thus creating boundaries and differentiation within the system.

III. Initial Statement
Through newscasts and movies, we are all familiar with the chain of command in the military. Each member has specific tasks and functions. If a member does not fulfill those functions, the whole organization could break down. This organization is also present in the family. Each member of a family has certain jobs to do. For example, as a new family, you have established a certain pattern for getting everyone to work and school on time. Linda, you are the general who has assigned Kim the responsibility of making the lunches, Keith the responsibility of dropping Ruth off at the babysitter's, and Anita the responsibility of washing the breakfast dishes. Linda, a part of your job is to make sure everything gets done. This morning pattern has become a part of your family organization. However, when Anita does not do her job, bypassing the chain of command, the morning pattern becomes chaotic. By this behavior, Anita is showing that she is upset with Linda's role in her new family and does not like the family organization.

IV. Follow-Up Techniques
Rules identification
Rules of interaction
Tickling of defenses

CONCEPT

Feedback Loops

I. Source
Based on Rosenblatt, P. (1994). *Metaphors of family systems theory.* New York: Guilford Press.

II. Brief Description
Feedback loops are the way family members communicate and process information in order to maintain equilibrium within the family system. They can be either negative or positive. Positive feedback loops promote change. Negative feedback loops inhibit change.

III. Initial Statement
Keith and Linda, as your family interacts, each member experiences feelings and beliefs. The communication of feelings and information creates a cycle of cause and effect within the family. You are each not only responding to present situations, but reacting according to the patterns of communication you have come to expect in your family. Each person's style of communication has developed as a result of many experiences in talking with other family members. These styles of communication have become very negative. My goal is to see whether we can replace them with positive styles.

IV. Follow-Up Techniques
Communication stances
Harmony among parts
Positive connotations

CONCEPT

First-Order Change

I. *Source*
Based on Hoffman, Lynn. (1981). *Foundations of family therapy.* New York: Basic Books.

II. *Brief Description*
First-order change involves ways of managing stress or conflict within the family. It represents corrective responses to small infractions that occur in the family system. These corrective responses can involve changing one member, modifying the family structure, revising the rules of the system, or creating a new rule.

III. *Initial Statement*
You have all agreed that you would like to live without all the yelling and screaming that goes on when there is conflict in the family. Let's come up with a different way for you to react to conflict. How about this: when someone hurts your feelings during an argument, you just hold up a hand, like this. This signal will remind the other person that his or her behavior is offensive to you, and you would like it to stop.

IV. *Follow-Up Techniques*
Challenging the communication
Formula task
Parallel examples

CONCEPT

Forgiveness

I. *Source*
Based on Augsburger, David. (1981). *Caring enough to forgive*. Scottdale, PA: Herald Press.

II. *Brief Description*
Forgiveness involves a rational process of confronting the pain of an injury and restructuring personal feelings and beliefs. The act of forgiveness consists of three phases: forgetting what lies in the past, recognizing what is taking place now, and reaching out to the future.

III. *Initial Statement*
Keith and Linda, you have been deeply hurt by people, especially those you love, and you cannot get past what happened until you forgive them. In order to begin the process, I want you to make a conscious decision to forgive. If this is impossible, at least make a decision not to seek revenge. At first, carrying out your decision will be hard; it takes time to feel forgiving. I want you to choose to take specific steps toward forgiveness. These steps involve forgetting what lies in the past, recognizing what is happening now, and reaching out to the future. If you make the decision now to forgive, you can begin to set yourself free of the injury.

IV. *Follow-Up Techniques*
Empty chair
Encouraging
Homework

CONCEPT

Fusion

I. *Source*
Based on Bowen, M. (1978). *Family therapy in clinical practice.* New York: Jason Aronson.

II. *Brief Description*
Fusion occurs when a family member becomes intellectually and emotionally overly involved in family relationships, to the point of never developing a sense of self—a personal identity with individual ideas, opinions, and values. Thus, the person lives life by rote, following values and beliefs adopted from others.

III. *Initial Statement*
Linda, you've told us you feel that you must attend all events that family and friends invite you to, even if you don't want to go. The thought of saying no brings up all kinds of guilt feelings in you. Usually, ideas with "should," "must," "always," or "never" attached are messages that you absorbed in childhood. Now that you are an adult, you can examine these ideas to see whether they make sense to you now. You need to take the time to develop your sense of what's important and come to your own conclusions about whether it makes sense to you to attend functions of family and friends.

IV. *Follow-Up Techniques*
Childhood home
Encouraging a response
Value assessment

CONCEPT

Helpfulness as Power

I. Source
Based on Madanes, C. (1981). *Strategic family therapy.* San Francisco: Jossey-Bass.

II. Brief Description
When one family member uses his or her influence to encourage the behavior of another member, the influenced family member experiences a feeling of power. That family member is fulfilling a role that is beneficial to the family member who has influenced the behavior. This kind of inter-action is displayed, for example, by a wife who feigns helplessness over finan-cial matters so that her husband, who is experiencing a loss of self-confidence, can take control of the situation and feel needed. In a similar way, children sometimes act out to get the family to refocus on different issues.

III. Initial Statement
Linda, sometimes when the children in a family witness a lot of tension and conflict, they try to distract the other family members to keep them from fighting. In this family, Kim and Mark are the two children who are at home the most and therefore feel the tension that is generated between you and Anita. When Kim and Mark see Anita and you fighting—and you, Keith, get-ting caught in the middle—Kim and Mark in turn begin to fight with each other. This causes all three of you—Linda, Keith, and Anita—to stop arguing and to direct your attention to Kim and Mark. Even though they risk being scolded or punished for their behavior, to them punishment is not a serious consequence compared to hearing their mom, stepdad, and older stepsister yell at one another. Through misbehaving, Kim and Mark stop the three of you from doing something that upsets and frightens them. In a sense, they have the power to end your arguments temporarily, which in turn gives them some relief from the anxiety they feel.

IV. Follow-Up Techniques
Family reconstruction
Quid pro quo
Use of self

CONCEPT

Homeostasis

I. *Source*
Based on Bedrosian, R., & Bozicas, G. (1994). *Treating family of origin problems: A cognitive approach.* New York: Guilford Press.

II. *Brief Description*
The family typically attempts to maintain the established pattern of behavior among its members, in what is called homeostasis. Most developmental changes challenge the family's homeostasis. Adjustments must be made in family rules, behavior, and interactions in order to cope with the changes. A well-functioning family makes the necessary adjustments to cope with change as well as maintain homeostasis.

III. *Initial Statement*
Keith and Linda, most of the time everyone works to maintain peace within the family. Everyone likes to know that family rules, routines, and relationships are going to stay pretty much the same from day to day and week to week. That continuity is not something we consciously think or worry about, but it does make us feel secure and comfortable. You can run into problems when changes take place so that everyday routines and rules don't seem to work any longer. When you try hard to make the old rules work, but they just don't, it might be time to adjust the rules. For example: Keith Jr., now that you are driving, you have new independence and responsibility. I'm sure this change has had an impact on family rules and routines. Are you picking the other kids up at school or taking them to events?

IV. *Follow-Up Techniques*
Expectations game
Reframing
Value assessment

CONCEPT

Humor

I. *Source*
Based on Napier, R. W., & Geshenfeld, M. K. (1987). *Groups: Theory and experience* (4th ed.). Boston: Houghton Mifflin.

II. *Brief Description*
Humor is hard to define but easy to recognize. It's a natural resource in families that can be scarce at times. Humor can make the intolerable, tolerable; the boring, bearable. Whether humor is spontaneous or staged, the good feelings and levity it provides give us much-needed perspective on our problems.

III. *Initial Statement*
Keith, sometimes we get so caught up in being serious that we miss the lighter side of life. Families in therapy often are very intense and serious during a session. But sometimes we need a break, to relax and get a new perspective on our problems. We want to be careful, though. Humor isn't healthy if it is used to hurt—that means no sarcasm and no put-downs.

IV. *Follow-Up Techniques*
Humor applied
Storytelling
Use of self

CONCEPT

Identified Patient

I. *Source*
Based on Goldenberg, H., & Goldenberg, I. (1994). *Counseling today's families* (2nd ed.) Pacific Grove, CA: Brooks/Cole.

II. *Brief Description*
The identified patient is the symptom bearer, who expresses a family's disequilibrium. The family identifies this person as their "primary concern."

III. *Initial Statement*
Your reason for starting therapy was that Linda has become frazzled, frustrated, and anxious. It's important for you to realize that this is not just Linda's problem, but a family problem. Linda's worries are probably just the tip of the iceberg. Somehow your family system has broken down, and Linda is expressing that fact. I'd like to talk about the frustrations you are all having with your relationships. Let's see if we can pinpoint where the system is breaking down.

IV. *Follow-Up Techniques*
Circular interview
Family secrets
Telegram

CONCEPT

Incongruent Communication

I. Source
Based on Satir, V. (1964). *Conjoint family therapy.* Palo Alto, CA: Science & Behavior Books.

II. Brief Description
Incongruent communication is a contradiction between what is said and how it is said or communicated. Often, we try to say the right thing with words, but what reveals our true feelings is the way we say it. This type of communication is often on an unconscious level and is met with a response that questions the sender's intention.

III. Initial Statement
I'm going to interrupt here and share what I see happening. Anita, although you have said that you wanted to listen to what Linda had to say, from looking at your body language, I don't think I believe you! The way you are slumped in your seat, with your arms crossed and your body turned away from Linda, is sending a different message. The message I'm receiving is that you really don't want to listen to Linda. Can you clear this up for me?

IV. Follow-Up Techniques
Dealing with anger
Empty chair *(for Anita first, then Linda)*
Worst alternative

CONCEPT

Incongruous Dual Hierarchy

I. *Source*
Based on Madanes, C. (1984). *Behind the one-way mirror: Advances in the practice of strategic therapy.* San Francisco: Jossey-Bass.

II. *Brief Description*
Incongruous dual hierarchy is a fancy term to describe an unusual power alignment within the family. For instance, children normally do not have as much power in a family as the adults or parents. But if a child develops an illness or behavior that the parents cannot control, the child then is in a more powerful position. For another example, a spouse who develops an illness is in a subordinate position to the other mate, who tries to help and protect. But because the mate cannot help or cure the partner who is ill, the "inferior" mate actually experiences a superior position.

III. *Initial Statement*
Linda, after your divorce from Al, your son Mark began wetting his bed. Mark has learned that when he wets the bed, you call Al, who then comes over to the house and spends time with him. Since the divorce, Mark has felt abandoned and lonely, and he needs reassurance and attention from both you and Al. His bed-wetting is a way of keeping both of you involved and focused on him. In a sense, his bed-wetting is controlling you and Al. That's a lot of power for a kid to have over his parents.

IV. *Follow-Up Techniques*
Reframing
Taking sides
Transactional patterns

CONCEPT

Interface Phenomena

I. Source
Based on Kantor, D., & Lehr, W. (1975). *Inside the family.* San Francisco: Jossey-Bass.

II. Brief Description
Every time a family system or subsystem meets, an interface occurs. At each interface, a family member responds on three subsystem levels: a personal level, an interpersonal level, and a familial level. Each level has different needs and obligations. When a message is incongruent, family members may respond to only part of the message.

III. Initial Statement
Keith and Linda, in family communications, we relate to one another all at once on three different levels: the personal, or "how I feel about this"; the interpersonal, or "how I feel about you and me"; and the familial, or "how I relate to you as a member of the whole family." Each position you communicate from has different needs and obligations. The message you intend to send may be confused because you're experiencing conflict about what needs and obligations you expect to be met on each level. When this happens, the individual you're talking to may also become confused and respond only to one level.

IV. Follow-Up Techniques
Boundaries
Motivation
Restructuring

CONCEPT

Interpersonal Functions

I. Source
Based on Alexander, J., & Parsons, B. V. (1982). *Functional family therapy.* Pacific Grove, CA: Brooks/Cole.

II. Brief Description
Behaviors within a family serve to encourage three interpersonal functions: merging, or achieving closeness; separating, or achieving independence; and midpointing, or achieving independence but maintaining close ties. The interpersonal function underlying a family's behavior can be identified by observing interactional sequences and attending to the thoughts and feelings expressed.

III. Initial Statement
Let's take a look at how your family's behavior affects your relationships. Keith Jr. is almost 16, becoming independent of the family. The arguments you have with him actually make it easier for him to separate from you. On the other hand, Kim's and Mark's arguments really pull you in. Arguments with Keith Jr. end in someone storming out, while the younger children's arguments end when Linda gets involved. Family behaviors can also help you balance your needs for closeness and independence, like leaving Anita in charge of Ruth. What examples can you come up with?

IV. Follow-Up Techniques
Boundaries
Reframing
Ropes

CONCEPT

Introjections

I. Source
Based on Strupp, H. H., & Binder, J. L. (1984). *Psychotherapy in a key.* New York: Basic Books.

II. Brief Description
Through our childhood interactions with our parents or parental figures, we develop patterns and expectations of future relationships. These patterns and expectations have considerable impact on our present-day relationships, especially those with significant others and therapists. Introjections are usually unconscious.

III. Initial Statement
Keith, you have described a feeling of emptiness in your relationships. Linda, you say that Keith rarely talks about his feelings and that this behavior is beginning to interfere with your relationship. When you describe your interactions as a child, Keith, you say that your parents never expressed feelings. They believed expressing feelings was a sign of weakness. When you expressed feelings, your parents would reprimand and chastise you. Keith, the way you learned to keep your feelings to yourself is now affecting your relationship with Linda.

IV. Follow-Up Techniques
Childhood home
Live history
Speaker's chair

CONCEPT

Ledger of Justice

I. Source
Based on Boszormenyi-Nagy, I., & Krasner, B. R. (1986). *Between give and take: A clinical guide to contextual therapy.* New York: Brunner/Mazel.

II. Brief Description
The ledger of justice has to do with the give-and-take process that exists in every relationship. The ledger is an ongoing assessment of the debt and credit one incurs in any two-way relationship. Often interaction within the dyad is motivated by an attempt to achieve a balance between debt and credit. The philosophy is "I'll scratch your back, you scratch mine."

III. Initial Statement
Linda, when you discuss the problems in your marriage, you often complain about the everyday tasks for which you alone are responsible, such as cooking and driving the kids to school. Keith, you say that you are overburdened with your work and with night school. You both feel you are being treated unfairly by being asked to do so much. You both seem to be keeping a record of what you give and what you get in return. It might be a good idea to explore this issue of fairness in what you give and get in your relationship. That way you can reach an agreement about what to expect from each other.

IV. Follow-Up Techniques
Monitoring
Person to person
Vulnerability contract

CONCEPT

Loyalty

I. Source

Based on Boszormenyi-Nagy, I. (1967). Relational modes and meaning. *Family therapy and disturbed families*. Palo Alto, CA: Science & Behavior Books.

II. Brief Description

In loyalty, a person prefers one person over another because of perceived worth or what the preferred person has done for the individual. In split loyalty, a person sees two people as equally important and is torn between them. Split loyalty is most often seen in families when a parent is pressured to devote more time to a child than to a spouse. Often, split loyalty leads to behavior problems.

III. Initial Statement

Keith and Linda, what I see occurring when the two of you fight about your marital problems is that Keith Jr. is pulled in to take sides. Keith Jr. wants to please both of you, and your asking him to choose between the two of you is too much for him to handle. He feels loyal to both of you, and you are asking him to be disloyal to one of you. The confusion is causing Keith Jr. to act out. What goes on between you two as husband and wife is not Keith Jr.'s concern or responsibility. You need to keep your problems between the two of you, and let Keith Jr. know that it's OK to love both of you, no matter what happens.

IV. Follow-Up Techniques

Awareness enhancement
Caring days
Harmony among parts

CONCEPT

Maturation

I. Source
Based on Satir, V. (1983). *Conjoint family therapy* (3rd ed.). Palo Alto, CA: Science & Behavior Books.

II. Brief Description
Maturation describes a stage of development in which a person masters self-control. Mature people accept responsibility for their behaviors and their outcomes. They make decisions based on accurate and realistic data. They express themselves directly to others while recognizing the uniqueness of each individual. Mature people deal with situations as they are rather than as they would like them to be.

III. Initial Statement
Linda and Anita, in order to enable both of you to have more control over yourselves, I would ask you to try a different way of responding to each other. I would like you, Linda, to confront Anita when she refuses to answer your questions, rather than complain to Keith about Anita's behavior. Additionally, I would ask you, Anita, to acknowledge Linda's question, even if only to say, "I don't want to tell you that." By accepting responsibility for your own behavior and its outcome—and dealing with the situation as it is and not as you'd like it to be—you have a better opportunity to increase your awareness of yourself, the other person, and the situation. These changes will also help you to experience a more satisfying level of control and avoid senseless arguments.

IV. Follow-Up Techniques
"I" statements
Self-disclosure
Siding

CONCEPT

Merited Trustworthiness

I. *Source*
Based on Boszormenyi-Nagy, I., with Krasner, B. R. (1986). *Between give and take: A clinical guide to contextual therapy.* New York: Brunner/Mazel.

II. *Brief Description*
Healthy families are characterized by mutual consideration of the true self-interests of each family member. Family members generally trust one another, based on the care and consideration each has shown for the other in the past. If an individual has earned trust by being trustworthy, that family member deserves it in the present and future.

III. *Initial Statement*
Linda, you and Anita have been having difficulty getting along right from the start of your relationship with Keith. In order to help you gain some insight into the situation, I'd like you to consider the idea of merited, or earned, trustworthiness. Anita may be having difficulty relating to you because she isn't sure whether you really care about her and whether she can really trust you. Linda, I'd like you to think about how you can show Anita that you care about her as an individual.

IV. *Follow-Up Techniques*
Crediting
Motivation
Value assessment

CONCEPT

Metacommunication

I. Source
Based on Bateson, G., Jackson, D., Haley, J., & Weakland, J. (1956). Toward a theory of schizophrenia. *Behavioral Science, 1,* 251–264.

II. Brief Description
Metacommunication is an abstract level of communication that carries an implied command or qualifying message. Each message that is communicated has two levels: content and affect. The first level states the content, such as "Wash your hands." The second level, affect, also carries a message, which may modify or qualify, reinforce or contradict the content. How the receiver should take the message is communicated nonverbally, with gestures, facial expression, posture, and intonation. Metacommunication influences and shapes family patterns, interactions, and rules.

III. Initial Statement
Keith and Linda, every time you talk to each other, you send underlying messages through your words. The words themselves mean something: they tell us what to do and give us information. A feeling and a message are also conveyed to us through your nonverbal cues. Let's pretend you said to your son, "Tell me about school today"—but as you said it, you never looked up from the paper you were reading. Your son heard the words, but he also received a second message from you. The metacommunication said, "I'm not really interested in hearing about school." That message didn't come from the words, but from the fact that you didn't look at your son when you spoke to him. If you really want to hear about the day, your metacommunication should convey that desire to your son; you could look up, sound enthusiastic, smile, and put the paper down.

IV. Follow-Up Techniques
Communication game
Rules identification
Rules of interaction

CONCEPT

Multigenerational Transmission

I. Source

Based on Bowen, M. (1976). Theory in the practice of psychotherapy. In P. J. Guerin (Ed.), *Family therapy: Theory and practice.* New York: Gardner Press.

II. Brief Description

Severe dysfunction in a family often is the result of the operation of the family's emotional system over several generations. In spousal selection, the same differentiation level is chosen, and at the same time the family projection process results in lower levels of self-differentiation for certain offspring. As each generation marries, a lowered level of differentiation may be passed on to the children. As each generation proceeds, the children are increasingly vulnerable to anxiety and fusion, in contrast to the experience of healthy families, in which children move toward a greater differentiation of self. The children are a product of the parents, who are the product of their own parents.

III. Initial Statement

We all know that hair and eye color can be passed on to the next generation. What you may not know is that your emotional state can also be carried from one generation to the next. What makes one person very emotional and another person not so emotional is the degree that a person can separate thoughts from feelings. If we can see the situation clearly even though we are upset, we handle stress better. For that reason, it is important to keep our cool when we feel like crying and getting angry. Everyone needs to be aware of tendencies to react in old patterns.

IV. Follow-Up Techniques

Childhood home
Expectations game
Systemic hypothesis

CONCEPT

Mystification

I. Source
Based on Laing, R. D. (1965). Mystification, confusion, and conflict. In
I. Boszormenyi-Nagy & J. L. Framo (Eds.), *Intensive family therapy: Theoretical
and practical aspects.* Hagerstown, MD: Harper & Row.

II. Brief Description
Mystification is used in an effort to avoid conflict and maintain the status
quo. Mystification clouds or masks over what a conflict is about, but does
not avoid it. Mystification involves invalidating (denying or negating) a person's interpretation of an experience. Usually, mystification involves a person's projecting his or her own feelings onto another.

III. Initial Statement
Keith, when Anita said she did not like the new house, the new school, or
her new family, you told her that she was "ungrateful, selfish, and crazy to
say that since the new house has a built-in pool." Your daughter stated her
feelings—her perception of the new home. Your response denies her feelings. Try to let go of your view of her position. Then listen to her perception
of the situation. You will then begin to get to the heart of the problem. Maybe
then the two of you will be able to discuss problems instead of shrouding
them and hoping that they go away by themselves.

IV. Follow-Up Techniques
Positive reinforcement
Unbalancing
Video playback

CONCEPT

Nuclear Family Emotional System

I. Source
Based on Bowen, M. (1978). *Family therapy in clinical practice.* New York: Jason Aronson.

II. Brief Description
The nuclear family emotional system is the emotional pattern seen in one generation of a particular family. From the time a couple meets to the time they marry, they develop emotional and communication patterns. The way they plan the period from dating to marriage tells a lot about what problems they may have as a couple. These patterns then continue on through the couple's children.

III. Initial Statement
In our day-to-day activities, we rarely take the time to think about why we react the way we do. It is just our nature to react to different things in particular ways. Linda and Keith, by observing yourselves individually and as a couple, you can find out a great deal from your responses to various events. By just taking the time to sit back and think about why you just yelled at the kids or why you just said such hateful things to each other, you are better able to come to terms with yourselves and your relationship.

IV. Follow-Up Techniques
Enactment
Metaphor
Transactional patterns

CONCEPT

Object Relations

I. Source
Based on Shaffer, D. (1993). *Developmental psychology: Childhood and adolescence* (3rd ed.). Pacific Grove, CA: Brooks/Cole.

II. Brief Description
Object relations describes the way an individual forms relationships based on experiences earlier in life. An individual's earlier experiences create certain expectations, which the person later searches for in relationships with significant others. Often, individuals become fixated in this early life experience, and they have difficulty in forming and maintaining relationships because they cannot separate expectation from reality.

III. Initial Statement
Linda, while discussing your previous marriage, you stated that one thing you disliked about Al was that he was too controlling. You also mentioned that you had to ask your father's permission for the smallest things. What I'm hearing now is that you want Keith to take a more active role in disciplining the children. Your past experiences seem to be dominated by the male figure in your life, and Keith's current indifference to the rules of the household seems to be disturbing you. How do you feel about my observation?

IV. Follow-Up Techniques
Childhood home
Enactment
Live history

CONCEPT

Paradigms

I. Source
Based on Haley, J. (1987). *Problem-solving therapy.* San Francisco: Jossey-Bass.

II. Brief Description
Each person in a marriage has brought to the union his or her own set of marital expectations and rules for family life. These paradigms must be retained for each person to have a sense of well-being, but the paradigm must also be modified to form a shared expectation so that the couple may have a life in common. A couple must be willing to compromise in order to form a new way of interacting with each other.

III. Initial Statement
Linda and Keith, you need to develop ways of doing things so that you can meet the needs of daily living without so much conflict. Among other things, you must figure out how to eat, sleep, have sex, fight, celebrate holidays, take vacations, spend money, pay bills, and do chores. In the early stages of a marriage, when there are no children, it is easier to be flexible about how and when things are done. As children arrive, a couple has less choice about how to do things. The couple must make a series of decisions about how to manage things as the family changes. In your case, Keith and Linda, you already have two ready-made families with past experiences concerning how things should be done. It will be harder for you, but you can make good decisions about how to meet daily needs. These decisions are the root of blending families.

IV. Follow-Up Techniques
Bathroom procedure
Homework
Rules indentification

CONCEPT

Parentification

I. *Source*
Based on Boszormenyi-Nagy, I., & Spark, G. M. (1973). *Intensive family therapy*. New York: Harper & Row.

II. *Brief Description*
Parentification is a child's assuming a parenting role temporarily or permanently. Usually, the child is quiet, conforming, and good. The parents are usually unable or unwilling to accept the parental role, and the family often has unexpressed rage, despair, and hostility. Illness, alcoholism, and desertion are frequently contributing factors.

III. *Initial Statement*
Linda and Keith, we seldom consider it a problem when a child heroically fills the role of a parent and does it well. However, fulfilling the role of parent too often may make the child grow up too fast and create a problem for the whole family. The adults feel guilty because they know that they have not been doing their job, and the whole family experiences a quiet depression and internal rage. Often, everyone is confused and doesn't know why.

IV. *Follow-Up Techniques*
Boundaries
Defining the problem
Pretend

CONCEPT

Parts to Be Played

I. Source
Based on Kantor, D., & Lehr, W. (1975). *Inside the family.* San Francisco: Jossey-Bass.

II. Brief Description
In many families, there are four basic parts to play: mover, follower, opposer, and bystander. When one family member takes some action, the other family members react. The one who initiates the action is the mover; those who react are co-movers. The co-movers may either follow, oppose, or be bystanders. These four basic parts allow us to perceive, understand, and conceptualize the various patterns of behavior in human systems.

III. Initial Statement
Keith and Linda, when one member of your family does something, the others react by taking on roles. Linda, when you get angry at Keith, you are the mover of the family. Each member of your family reacts to you in one way or another. Kim and Mark fulfill the role of follower by backing you up. Anita and Keith are the opposers, because they challenge your anger. Keith Jr. acts as a bystander by not taking sides. Each of you can take different roles in different situations. Looking at who takes what roles and when can help you start to understand your family.

IV. Follow-Up Techniques
Anatomy of a relationship
Systemic hypothesis
Sculpting

CONCEPT

Power in the Family

I. *Source*

Haley, J. (1976). *Problem-solving therapy: New strategies for effective family therapy*. San Francisco: Jossey-Bass.

II. *Brief Description*

Power in the family involves family members' struggle to secure the position of rule maker. The main issue is who is in charge. Parents should generate the rules in a family, but often children step in if their parents cannot make rules. Conflict over family power may continue well into a child's adult life.

III. *Initial Statement*

Keith and Linda, you seem to be at a stalemate when it comes to disciplining the children. You each say that your approach is the most effective, and each of you disciplines your way. Your children are receiving mixed signals; they are confused, so they create their own rules. Whether you go with one method or you compromise, Keith and Linda, it is important to make a decision to act together.

IV. *Follow-Up Techniques*

Negotiated quiet time
Parallel examples
Past successes

CONCEPT

Projective Identification

I. Source
Based on Brems, C. (1993). *A comprehensive guide to child psychotherapy.* Boston: Allyn & Bacon.

II. Brief Description
Unrealistic expectations, carried over from childhood, occur in the lives of most people with relationship difficulties. Projective identifications are unfulfilled expectations of childhood carried into a marital situation, where it is believed the missing experience can be supplied. These expectations are rarely conscious and may be experienced as a longing that cannot be satisfied.

III. Initial Statement
Keith and Linda, when you were children, you probably had expectations of your families that they did not fulfill. Now, as adults, you have brought these expectations into your marriage. What I see is two people who are playing the role of parents and at the same time trying desperately to have your expectations fulfilled. Keith and Linda, let's look at those unmet needs and see how they are affecting your expectations of each other.

IV. Follow-Up Techniques
Caring days
Childhood home
Logical and natural consequences

CONCEPT

Psychological Distance

I. *Source*
Based on Minuchin, S., & Fishman, H. C. (1981). *Family therapy techniques.*
Cambridge, MA: Harvard University Press.

II. *Brief Description*
Often, the way family members sit in a session provides clues about their
affiliations. A therapist should be aware of spatial indicators as well as verbal patterns that occur when a particular family member is talking. The concept of psychological distance can help the therapist understand relationships
among family members based on visual and verbal data patterns, not simply
the content of what is said.

III. *Initial Statement*
Kim, since we have been working together, you have said very little unless
I talked directly to you. In both sessions you have pushed your chair closer
to your mother and have chosen a seat that is not near Keith. Tell me about
sitting so far away from Keith. *(After Kim speaks, continue.)* You have all
chosen the same places as in our first session. Think about the way you are
sitting and whom you choose to sit near. What does this say about the family
members you feel closest to?

IV. *Follow-Up Techniques*
Family choreography
Family drawings
Video playback

CONCEPT

Punctuation

I. Source

Based on Watzlawick, P., Beavin, J. H., & Jackson, D. (1967). *Pragmatics of human communication.* New York: Norton.

II. Brief Description

Punctuation in communication involves the complex circular interaction of a family dialogue in which each person believes that what he or she says is caused by what the other person said. An impasse is created in these circumstances because one person punctuates a sequence of interactions so that it appears as though the other person has the power. As long as the participants look at the dialogue as a linear, cause-and-effect communication, they will continue to punctuate it so they can place blame.

III. Initial Statement

Let's examine what I hear as the two main lines of dialogue between you. Linda, you keep saying that you nag Keith only because he withdraws from you. At the same time, Keith, you say you withdraw because Linda nags. You both believe that the other person is causing the problem, so you can't solve it. As long as you both continue to place blame on the other person, you're going to keep going around in circles, each of you waiting for the other person to change. The situation is like your kids' having a fight and yelling: "He started it." "No, she started it." It really doesn't matter who caused it. The important thing is to make a change and start to resolve the conflict.

IV. Follow-Up Techniques

Communication game
Looking
Unbalancing

CONCEPT

Quid pro Quo

I. Source

Based on Jackson, D. (1977). The study of the family. In *The interactional view: Studies at the Mental Health Research Institute, Palo Alto, 1965–1974.* New York: Norton.

II. Brief Description

Quid pro quo literally means "something for something" and describes the process of reciprocation that occurs in relationships. Family quid pro quo involves the expectations each person has of the others concerning the rules of the relationship and who is responsible for making them. These terms may fluctuate throughout a relationship, but when they are amicably worked out, quid pro quo can be thought of as a family's standard level of functioning as a unit.

III. Initial Statement

Keith and Linda, you each have expectations for the other people in your family. It would be good for each of you to realize that you are working on a set of rules for your relationships. These rules include who makes the rules and what the rules are. You each make deals in order to get at least some of the rules you want. Let's talk about some of your deals.

IV. Follow-Up Techniques

Contingency contract
Expectations game
Quid pro quo

CONCEPT

Reciprocity

I. Source

Based on Brown, J., & Christensen, D. (1986). *Family therapy: Theory and practice*. Pacific Grove, CA: Brooks/Cole.

II. Brief Description

When one partner takes on most or even all family responsibilities while the other plays the irresponsible counterpart, reciprocity is more than adequate for one and less than adequate for the other. Fused together, the two pseudo-selves develop an arrangement in which one partner functions less and less well while the other takes up the slack by assuming responsibility for them both. Both partners are involved, and both must choose to alter the pattern for effective change to occur.

III. Initial Statement

This situation with Keith's coworker does seem to be troublesome. Yet I notice that you, Linda, seem to be expressing all of the frustration and anger. Keith, I don't see you expressing any emotion at all. Sometimes couples get caught in a pattern where one person expresses all the feeling for both of them. The other person may not feel the need to be expressive, because enough emotion is already being expressed for the two of them. Do either of you see yourselves in this picture?

IV. Follow-Up Techniques

Communication game
Family choreography
Unbalancing

CONCEPT

Relational Ethics

I. Source
Based on Boszormenyi-Nagy, I., & Ulrich, D. (1981). Contextual family therapy. In A. S. Gurman & D. F. Kniskern (Eds.), *Handbook of family therapy.* New York: Brunner/Mazel.

II. Brief Description
Relational ethics is the balance of fairness in the distribution of merits, benefits, and burdens among people over the long term, in which the interests of each are considered by the others. The study of the relational ethics of a client is most beneficially accomplished in a multigenerational approach to therapy.

III. Initial Statement
Keith and Linda, each of you brought to your marriage some idea of what would be a fair distribution of the burdens and benefits of your life together. It seems now that you disagree on what a fair distribution looks like. You probably got your ideas from some combination of what you learned as children in your families and what you learned in your relationships with your first spouses. It would be wise to look at those earlier relationships to see how your original ideas of fairness are causing conflict in your present relationships.

IV. Follow-Up Techniques
Childhood home
Family reconstruction
Multidirected partiality

CONCEPT

Rituals

I. *Source*

Based on Jacobs, J., & Wolin, S. (1989, July/August). Ritual strengthening. *The Family Therapy Networker,* pp. 41–45.

II. *Brief Description*

Rituals are an important part of family life. Rituals incorporate family values and a sense of identity. Many family rituals are created around holidays, birthdays, meals, and joint activities. Family rituals are disturbed by alcoholic behavior, physical or mental illness, divorce, and death. The creation of family rituals in blended families signifies the family's maturing.

III. *Initial Statement*

We've been working together for a number of weeks, and I've learned a lot about your family. One thing that stands out in my mind is that your family has very few rituals. Family rituals can involve dinnertime, family celebrations of special occasions and holidays, vacations, and so on. These times are very important in the development of family values and closeness. We are going to work on strengthening your family's rituals. It will be very important for your family to incorporate past experiences so that both parts of the family can begin to feel ownership of the rituals as one unit. Let's see what the children's favorite times are now.

IV. *Follow-Up Techniques*

Fighting fair
Photos
Value assessment

CONCEPT

Roles

I. Source
Based on Satir, V. (1972). *Peoplemaking,* Palo Alto, CA: Science & Behavior Books.

II. Brief Description
Individual members of a family are linked together in various ways. One way to examine the family network is in terms of basic family roles. When each person's roles are identified, it becomes easier to map out both the connections and the conflicts that can exist. Family roles are very different from family to family, and each child tends to carry his or her role to adulthood.

III. Initial Statement
Each of the seven of you is an individual. You're a single person who is special and unique in the world. You're also connected to the other people in your family, in special ways. One way you're linked is in pairs, and each different pair has a role name. Some of these family pairs are husband and wife, father and daughter, mother and son, brother and brother, and sister and brother. We all have our ideas of what our own role is, and we also have ideas about what other people's roles are. Mark, you have your own ideas about your roles: a son and a brother. You also have your own ideas of what it means to be a mother or a sister, even though that's not who you are. There can be a problem if two people see the same role in two different ways. Let's say that Mark thinks that mothers are always supposed to do things for their sons, but Linda thinks that moms should help their kids by teaching them to do certain things for themselves. So Mark thinks Linda's role is one thing, and Linda thinks her role is something else. Rather than thinking about who's right and who's wrong, let's figure out whether each of you has a different idea about what a mom's role or job is. When you can talk over your ideas about what each person's family role is, it's easier to figure out why you feel confused or angry when people behave differently.

IV. Follow-Up Techniques
Family choreography
Rejunction
Sculpting

CONCEPT

Rules

I. *Source*
Based on Jackson, D. D. (1965). Family rules: The marital quid pro quo. *Archives of General Psychiatry, 12,* 589.

II. *Brief Description*
Families can learn a great deal about their family systems when they examine their own family rules and how these rules operate in governing the system. Families establish both spoken and unspoken rules. Exploring the family's overt and covert rules can make it easier to identify stress-producing situations that may result in dysfunctional patterns.

III. *Initial Statement*
A family is like a small factory or a tiny city. The factory or the city government is run by a set of rules, which everyone is supposed to follow so that things go well. Families have rules too, but we don't often think about exactly what these rules are. Some rules are very clear, and everyone in your family knows them: Put your dirty clothes in the hamper. Don't feed the dog at the dinner table. Cover your mouth when you cough. Do you have rules like those? Some rules we figure out by ourselves: Don't bother Dad until he's been home from work for at least an hour. Some rules are not so clear, and we hardly ever talk about them. Because we don't talk about a rule, not everyone understands it. Mark thinks the rule means one thing, and Kim thinks it means something else. It can be very confusing when you don't know what the rules are, or if you think you're not allowed to ask questions about the rules. I'd like all of you to begin thinking about what your family rules are.

IV. *Follow-Up Techniques*
Rules identification
Rules of interaction
Straightforward directives

CONCEPT

Scapegoating

I. Source
Based on Worden, M. (1994). *Family therapy basics*. Pacific Grove, CA: Brooks/Cole.

II. Brief Description
Parents experiencing conflict or stress may form a triangle with a child, because the child's involvement may direct attention away from the conflict. Scapegoating is one form or path this triangulation may take. The parents and the child join together in eliciting acting-out behavior from the child. The child's acting-out behavior draws the parents' attention away from their marital stress, as they join forces to attempt to deal with their problem child. The scapegoat may serve to relieve stress within the family, but at the expense of the child's long-term adjustment and personality.

III. Initial Statement
Keith and Linda, a family therapist often looks beyond the initial concern or problem when dealing with a child who has behavior problems. While there are lots of things to look at and questions to ask, one important question we should ask is what purpose this behavior serves in this family. It is quite common for parents experiencing problems or conflict in their relationship to unknowingly draw a child into their situation. Their attention is then diverted from the marital problem, and the parents join together in an effort to control the child. In a way, the child is actually protecting the parents through his or her behavior problems. Linda, do you see this happening in your family with Anita?

IV. Follow-Up Techniques
Defining the problem
Detriangling
Triangles

CONCEPT

Second-Order Change

I. *Source*
Based on Watzlawick, P., Weakland, J. E., & Richard, F. (1974). *Change: Principles of problem formation and problem resolution.* New York: Norton.

II. *Brief Description*
A family member cannot resolve a problem by continually changing the rules. For real change to take place, the structure of the system must be changed. This second-order change involves transforming the way the situation is viewed. The family member needs to look at, think about, and understand the problem from a different frame of reference. No rules or roles need to be created; behaviors change because of the family member's altered view.

III. *Initial Statement*
Keith, you know that there's a difference between changing behaviors and changing attitudes. A change in behavior may be only a surface change, with nothing underneath being any different. For example, a husband is upset because his wife seems to be spending more time going out with friends than spending time with him. She isn't doing anything special with him. If she sat home once or twice a week with him, she would be changing her behavior. She would be changing her attitude if she realized that her husband is lonely and would like to join her when she goes out, and so she invited him to join her on one of her outings. She would be spending time with her husband while doing something special and would actually change the way she perceives the problem. She would begin to see her husband as lonely instead of as a nagging spouse.

IV. *Follow-Up Techniques*
Positive double bind
Telegram
Touch

CONCEPT

Self-Esteem

I. Source
Based on Thompson, C., & Rudolph, L. (1992). *Counseling children* (3rd ed.). Pacific Grove, CA: Brooks/Cole.

II. Brief Description
Self-esteem is a person's sense of worthiness: the integration of one's confidence, respect for oneself, and sense of competence as a person. Our self-esteem affects each relationship we have, because our self-esteem determines what we are willing to try to do within a relationship.

III. Initial Statement
Keith and Linda, a positive self-esteem is something that all parents desire for their children. But what does it really mean? To me, it means having self-confidence and self-respect, and treating others as though they deserve the same. I see those qualities as basic to being a healthy person or a healthy family, and I will encourage the growth of self-esteem in our sessions.

IV. Follow-Up Techniques
Encouraging
Focus on strengths
Positive connotations

CONCEPT

Shame

I. Source
Based on Hemfelt, R., Minirth, F., & Meier, P. (1991). *We are driven*. Nashville: Thomas Nelson Publishers.

II. Brief Description
Shame is a response to exposure and compels the exposed person to hide not only physically but emotionally. When people are violated or exposed, they remember past experiences of shame along with the present situation. This layering of shame causes people to think they're unworthy, dirty, out of control, or in need of punishment. When people feel shame, they may react by blushing, averting their eyes, lowering their head, or withdrawing completely.

III. Initial Statement
Linda, I see you hang your head and look at the floor as though you wish it would swallow you up. I think you're feeling ashamed, which is one of the hardest feelings to talk about. Shame usually comes about when the very core of who we are is violated, and it can cause us to feel that we're no good, bad, or dirty. Shame tells us that we deserve to be punished, even though we don't. Perhaps you remember other times in the past when you felt similar shame, and you may want to just pretend it didn't happen. As children, even though we may be unable to control what happens to us, it still may make us feel a sense of shame. If you can remember how you dealt with these feelings in the past, we may be able to work through your present pain.

IV. Follow-Up Techniques
Childhood home
Defining the problem
Use of self

CONCEPT

Sibling Positions

I. Source
Based on Bowen, M. (1978). *Family concept in clinical practice.* New York: Jason Aronson.

II. Brief Description
In accordance with their birth order, people take on certain familial and social roles, which in turn shape their personality and sense of self. Certain traits are characteristic of each position: for example, the firstborn is typically overachieving. Each of us carries these traits into adulthood, and they can contribute to marital conflicts.

III. Initial Statement
Keith and Linda, I would like to talk about something that I think may be familiar to each of you. We have all seen how the last-born child often remains the baby of the family, and how the firstborn is usually the responsible and overachieving type. While you may be familiar with these ideas, you may not have thought about the powerful part your own birth-order positions play in your lives. Basically, the idea is that important personality traits follow from the sibling position in which a person grows up. Of course, we are not responsible for our birth-order positions, but it might be a good idea at this point to look at how you, Keith, as the oldest, and you, Anita, as the middle child, might be contributing to Mark's tantrums just by assuming the roles into which you were born.

IV. Follow-Up Techniques
Family choreography
Family drawings
Family reconstruction

CONCEPT

Split Loyalties

I. *Source*
Based on Berg-Cross, L. (1988). *Basic concepts in family therapy: An introductory text*. New York: Haworth Press.

II. *Brief Description*
The concept of split loyalties describes a pattern in which the child is caught between the parents. Both parents want the child to side with them against the other parent, thus placing the child in a no-win situation. This problem often arises before a separation or divorce, when each parent strives to obtain the child's favor or attention by putting the other parent down. Adolescents in this situation often panic and resort to measures that outrage both parents, such as running away, using drugs, or engaging in vandalism. Initially, this type of behavior strengthens the mutual dyad, since it creates a mutual concern on the part of the parents. Unfortunately, the conflict between the parents resumes once the parental coalition is effective in reducing the child's problem.

III. *Initial Statement*
Let's examine Ruth's disruptive behavior a little more closely. Keith and Linda, I have observed that the two of you are constantly disagreeing with each other. When you disagree, you each try to win Ruth's attention and favor for your side. Competing for her favor hasn't helped Ruth, and neither of you has won her attention. In fact, you are hurting her. She is now afraid to express care or concern for either of you. Instead, she is reacting by developing behavior problems, in the hope that the two of you will pull together instead of pulling her apart. Even though the two of you are having difficulties, you both care for Ruth, and she cares for each of you. You can't expect Ruth to take one side; she will try to be loyal to both sides.

IV. *Follow-Up Techniques*
Homework prescriptions
Triadic exercises
Vulnerability contract

CONCEPT

Strategies

I. Source
Based on Kantor, D., & Lehr, W. (1975). *Inside the family.* San Francisco: Jossey-Bass.

II. Brief Description
Family strategies are consistent patterns of interactions whose purpose is to allow each family member to achieve his or her own goals. Strategies typically fall into one of three categories: maintenance, stress, and repair. Each member has an understanding of the strategy and knows how to play his or her part.

III. Initial Statement
Linda and Keith, what I see happening in your family is a conflict in the way you are operating. Whenever a new family is formed, it is necessary to work through the way each member is expected to function. The goals of the new family must be taken into consideration so that no one is denied access to his or her goals. In your case, Keith and Linda, you have formed a new family from two preexisting ones. The children are unsure about how they should function and how their needs will be met. It may be helpful to sit down with everyone for a family meeting to discuss just what everybody wants and how everyone's needs will be fulfilled.

IV. Follow-Up Techniques
Crediting
Defining the problem
Rejunction

CONCEPT

Subsystems

I. *Source*
Based on Brown, J., & Christensen, D. (1986). *Family therapy: Theory and practice.* Pacific Grove, CA: Brooks/Cole.

II. *Brief Description*
Families usually consist of several coexisting subsystems. Subsystems may track generation, sex, interests, or functions. Within the family system, some subsystems have more power than others. In functional families, a hierarchy of power exists, with the parental subsystem at the top of the hierarchy. As the children in a family grow, many different kinds of subsystems form, including such groups as workers, music lovers, gardeners, and readers.

III. *Initial Statement*
Keith and Linda, within your family and all families, there are special groupings of people that we can call subsystems. Mother and father form one subsystem; the children form another. Mother and daughter form a special group, as do father and son. Two brothers may form a special group based on an interest such as in baseball. These subsystems are important to your life as a family, and they serve many purposes. One important job of the mother and father group is to protect and watch over the rest of the family. In order to do this, Mom and Dad must have the most power, and the last say when issues come up. Families can't always work as democracies, with everyone having an equal say. They work best when Mom and Dad listen to the other members but still have the final say.

IV. *Follow-Up Techniques*
Challenging the structure
Siding
Triangles

CONCEPT

Success Identity

I. Source
Based on Glasser, W. (1976). *Positive addiction.* New York: Harper & Row.

II. Brief Description
Success identity is a state in which people perceive themselves as able to receive and give love, feel they are significant with respect to others, and have a strong sense of self-worth. People in this state do not meet their needs at the expense of others. This attitude or outlook can be achieved by first choosing something you enjoy doing, like running, walking, or meditation, and doing it repeatedly until you are good at it. Once achieved, this success carries over into other areas of your personality, creating a success identity.

III. Initial Statement
You know, when you're really good at something, you feel good about yourself. Creating this feeling requires that you choose something that you would like to do regularly, like running, walking, or meditation—something that you can commit yourself to, creating a positive addiction. I'd like each of you to make a commitment to practice one thing every day for a month. Not only will this practice make you better at whatever you choose to do, every day you'll be reminding yourself of how special you are. Anita, I know you could really use a shot of feeling special. What's something you like that's good for you?

IV. Follow-Up Techniques
Family council
Paradoxical prescription
Positive reinforcement

CONCEPT

Symptom as a Metaphor

I. Source

Based on Madanes, C. (1981). *Strategic family therapy.* San Francisco: Jossey-Bass.

II. Brief Description

A symptom (the behavior that is a problem for a family) may be manifested by only one member, but it symbolically represents the behavior or internal state of the family system as a whole. In this way, words or actions can have many levels of meaning beyond what is apparent. A child's stomachache on Monday morning may represent his own anxiety about going to school and his mother's anxiety about seeing him go. It may also symbolize the general tension in the house as parents gear up to return to their weekday schedule.

III. Initial Statement

You know, Keith and Linda, sometimes a family member has really powerful radar that picks up the feelings of other family members, even if those feelings are hidden. That family member then bounces those feelings back in all kinds of ways. Those feelings can come out as stomachaches, grouchiness, or even a tendency to be accident-prone like Mark here! I'm wondering whether Mark's numerous accidents since your remarriage might be signs of his feelings of anger and hurt.

IV. Follow-Up Techniques

Awareness enhancement
Metaphor
Transactional patterns

CONCEPT

System of Interaction as a Metaphor

I. *Source*

Based on Madanes, C. (1981). *Strategic family therapy.* San Francisco: Jossey-Bass.

II. *Brief Description*

In a relationship, when two people always take the same stance or assume the same role, these behaviors become rigid patterns of interaction. This way of relating is often reflected in the way the two people deal with each other regarding the presenting problem; the same way of relating can be mirrored in other relationships within the system. Thus one mode of interacting serves as a metaphor for another. By addressing in therapy the pattern of interaction in one relationship, the other relationship is affected indirectly.

III. *Initial Statement*

Sometimes a specific difficulty can be symbolic of something broader. Relationships get into trouble not because of a particular problem, but because of the way we deal with each other about the problem. Listening to you talk about the issues facing your family, Keith, I've noticed that whenever Linda tries to say something, you ignore her comments. I've also noticed that when your children try to tell a story, Linda, you criticize their way of telling it. I suspect that the level of tension in the family that brought you here might change dramatically if even one of you practices listening without interrupting or criticizing when another family member speaks. Small changes can have a big impact. Who wants to volunteer?

IV. *Follow-Up Techniques*

Anatomy of a relationship
Person to person
Video playback

CONCEPT

Target Dimensions

I. *Source*
Based on Kantor, D., & Lehr, W. (1975). *Inside the family.* San Francisco: Jossey-Bass.

II. *Brief Description*
Target dimensions are specific life goals that family members attempt to achieve. These broader life goals include having love, some control, and real meaning in one's life. These goals are worked out through the interactional behaviors of family members as they seek their target dimensions.

III. *Initial Statement*
I have noticed that each member of your family strives to achieve certain goals. As you interact, you show other members what your goals are. Generally, everyone wants to obtain the feeling of love and being loved, the freedom to decide and to get what one wants in life, and a way to explain reality and define one's identity. In your family, Keith and Linda, I sense a struggle among family members in trying to obtain goals. It seems as if you each are struggling with a different goal. In an ideal situation, everyone would be able to obtain all of these goals.

IV. *Follow-Up Techniques*
Crediting
Ordeals
Use of self

CONCEPT

Time

I. Source
Based on Snider, M. (1992). *Process family therapy.* Boston: Allyn & Bacon.

II. Brief Description
Time together as a family involves activities that include everyone in the family. These activities might also include family friends who share the same interests or values. Spending time together can be as simple as eating dinner together or as dramatic as taking a once-in-a-lifetime trip. Participating in some kind of cultural, social, or outdoor activity together helps a family become healthy and strong.

III. Initial Statement
Keith, sharing time together as a family and with special family friends builds a bond that will last. In listening to your daily schedules, I did not hear about many times when all of you were together. Keith, you work from 3 to 11 p.m. at the factory. Linda works from 7 a.m. to 3 p.m., so she can be home when the children get home from school. On the weekends, Keith Jr. works part-time. During the week, Kim and Mark stay after school for clubs, and Linda has to drop them off and pick them up. That means Anita is left alone with Ruth most of the afternoon. Maybe eating breakfast together during the week or spending one weekend afternoon as a family, having a cookout with family and friends or going on some kind of family outing, will make the family bond stronger.

IV. Follow-Up Techniques
Detriangling
Humor applied
Triadic exercises

CONCEPT

Time Cable

I. Source

Based on Hoffman, L. (1983). Diagnosis and assessment in family therapy: II. A co-evolutionary framework for systemic family therapy. *Family Therapy Collections, 4,* 35–61. Rockville, MD: Aspen Systems.

II. Brief Description

The time cable is a method that allows us to examine how a presenting problem has evolved over time. Each family member is asked to discuss the problem within the following time frames: present (here and now), onset (when the problem first occurred), historical (prior to onset), and future.

III. Initial Statement

Keith, in order to get a better understanding of a problem—its impact and how it may be handled in the future—it is often helpful to look at the situation from a time-related perspective. For example, to look at the problem between Linda and Anita within this context, I would ask the following questions of each of you: What is the problem like right now? What was it like when it first started, and how has it changed from then to now? What was it like before the problem started, and how do you think it might be in the future? Do you remember any problem like this in your parents' or grandparents' experience?

IV. Follow-Up Techniques

Humor applied
Live history
Marital schism

CONCEPT

Triangulation

I. *Source*
Based on Atwood, J. (1992). *Family therapy: A systemic-behavioral approach.*
Chicago: Nelson-Hall Publishers.

II. *Brief Description*
When a two-person system is placed under stress, there is a tendency for
one member of the dyad to pull in a vulnerable third person, to create a
triangle. This triangulation helps restore stability by lowering stress and
anxiety levels. However, the triangulated person is kept dependent and un-
differentiated. A therapist can create a triangle with a dyad as he or she
works with the mother and father in a family, so that they "triangle" on to
the therapist. This reduces the stress in the marital relationship without involving a child (usually the most likely candidate for triangulation). Triangles
become the basic building blocks in a family's system.

III. *Initial Statement*
When people in a relationship are either too close or too distant, generating
stress or anxiety, they often recruit a third person, so that the emotions
created by the stress overflow on that person. This third person, often a child,
has the least sense of self in the family and is prevented from growing further as a person because of the dependency created by the triangle. The
third person adds a dimension that refocuses the relationship between the
original pair. Keith and Linda, you might disagree about how to deal with
Mark's learning problem. An intense relationship may then form between
Linda and Mark, as you, Linda, become more and more frustrated with Keith's
point of view and more sympathetic with Mark's struggles. Your sympathy
with Mark distances Keith, cooling your original conflict. Have you seen this
happen?

IV. *Follow-Up Techniques*
Defining the problem
Psychodrama
Triangles

CONCEPT

Worldview

I. Source
Based on Hanna, S., & Brown, J. (1995). *The practice of family therapy: Key elements across models.* Pacific Grove, CA: Brooks/Cole.

II. Brief Description
Families provide individuals with a sense of identity and belonging. Families encourage the production of shared constructs and ways of viewing the world. Expectations affect behavior, reinforcing themselves in self-fulfilling prophecies. Families are at all points along the continuum of illness to health. The worldview that each family brings to therapy determines to a great degree how the work will proceed. True systems therapy addresses these expectancies of the world that families bring to the treatment room.

III. Initial Statement
Keith and Linda, each family is at a different point on the continuum of feelings. At one end, families may have a pessimistic view of the world as a threatening place where there is no trust. Further along the continuum, families have a threatening view of the world as a place where outside people cannot be trusted because they are against the family. At the other end of the continuum, families take a positive view of the world, as a nurturing place with caring people ready to help if asked. Let's talk about how you two see your family on this continuum.

IV. Follow-Up Techniques
Behavioral rehearsal
Focus on strengths
Self-disclosure

PART TWO

TECHNIQUES

TECHNIQUE

Anatomy of a Relationship

I. Source
Based on Satir, V., & Baldwin, M. (1983). *Satir step by step: A guide to creating change in families.* Palo Alto, CA: Science & Behavior Books.

II. Brief Description
Every marriage is a contract, whether verbal or written. A therapist can draw out that contract by creating a sculpture. Each person has a chance to look at the therapist's perception of their relationship and then to share their own perceptions of the experience with one another.

III. Initial Statement
Keith and Linda, both of you have created a relationship that is like a contract within your marriage. This contract has Linda needing someone strong to lean on. That someone is you, Keith. I'm going to ask her to stand behind you and lean against you. We will have a chance to examine how the two of you feel about this physical contact.

IV. Concluding Statement
By examining Linda's need to lean on you, Keith has shared the feelings that crossed through his mind. As we changed this experience to a more extreme state, Keith did express his feelings.

V. Guideline
Role playing

TECHNIQUE

Awareness Enhancement

I. *Source*
Based on Satir, V., & Baldwin, M. (1983). *Satir step by step: A guide to creating change in families.* Palo Alto, CA: Science & Behavior Books.

II. *Brief Description*
Awareness of feelings helps us to communicate clearly. To enhance awareness, the therapist uses triadic exercises, in which two people engage in an interaction and a third observes. The third person then offers feedback on the interaction to the first two people.

III. *Initial Statement*
Keith, Linda, and Anita, we are going to concentrate for a while on becoming more aware of feelings in others and in ourselves. When we become aware of feelings, communication is clearer. The two of you, Keith and Linda, will have a conversation for five minutes, while Anita observes. At the end of the time, Anita can talk about what feelings she was able to see, how these feelings were communicated, and how she felt not being a part of the conversation. You two, Keith and Linda, will then be asked to share your experiences. The rest of the family will just watch for now.

IV. *Concluding Statement*
I hope that becoming more aware of each of your feelings is more important to you now. Anita's telling you how you convey your messages can help you choose to make changes. Also, interaction in families is not always an interaction just between two people. Sometimes three or more people are involved in a conversation. I hope this exercise has given you a chance to see how you feel in this family, especially how you feel about different ways of being ignored.

V. *Guideline*
Group leadership skills

TECHNIQUE

Bathroom Procedure

I. *Source*

Based on Brock, G. W., & Barnard, C. P. (1988). *Procedures in family therapy.* Boston: Allyn & Bacon.

II. *Brief Description*

The bathroom procedure is used to enhance the parent alliance, especially in disciplining of children. The therapist and parents leave the consultation room and use a nearby bathroom to discuss how they are going to handle the children. The therapist helps them decide on a course of action that they will carry out during the rest of the session. Upon returning to the session, the children are asked to act up again, and the parents are asked to act on their agreement. Parents are then encouraged to use the bathroom at home for their discussions whenever the children require guidance.

III. *Initial Statement*

Linda, you have been expressing your frustration over having to do much of the disciplining yourself, and Keith, you are concerned that your wife is too easy with the children. Despite each of your interventions, Kim has continued to hit or push her brother. Let's take the next five minutes or so to discuss how you can handle Kim's behavior. It's important for us to have privacy, so we're going to leave the children here. They'll be fine for the short time we'll be gone, and we'll use the bathroom in the waiting room.

IV. *Concluding Statement*

It seems that disciplining Kim in a way that you both were comfortable with, had a stronger effect on Kim's behavior. Now that you each have a pretty good idea of the bathroom procedure, I want you and your wife to use your own bathroom at home to discuss ways of handling Kim when she is out of control.

V. *Guideline*

Discipline

TECHNIQUE

Behavioral Rehearsal

I. Source
Based on Thompson, C., & Rudolph, L. (1992). *Counseling children* (3rd ed.). Pacific Grove, CA: Brooks/Cole.

II. Description
Behavioral rehearsal is practicing a new behavior in a safe environment before actually attempting the behavior in the real world. This technique allows a person to obtain feedback and develop confidence in performing the behavior.

III. Initial Statement
Linda and Anita, I've noticed that when you try to communicate with each other, you yell or use sarcasm most of the time. I would like to see the two of you communicate by respectfully listening to each other, speaking in calm voices, and responding only after the other has finished speaking. Now I want the two of you to engage in a conversation using these guidelines.

IV. Concluding Statement
You have both seen that it is possible for the two of you to communicate without the yelling or sarcasm. It would really help if you continue to follow these guidelines at home.

V. Guideline
Behavioral rehearsal

TECHNIQUE

Boundaries

I. Source

Based on Minuchin, S., & Fishman, H. (1981). *Family therapy techniques.* Cambridge, MA: Harvard University Press.

II. Brief Description

Boundaries clear communication limits that are defined and set during the session. The therapist attempts to provide a psychological distance within the family subsystem by bringing certain behaviors to the family's attention. These boundaries are intended to be implemented outside of therapy.

III. Initial Statement

Anita, I noticed that before you answered questions about your mother, you looked at your father. Keith, I also noticed that you often finish Anita's sentences for her when she pauses. Anita, for the rest of the session, I'd like you to move your chair so that you're facing your mother and can't see your father's face. Keith, I'm going to ask you just to listen to my discussion with Linda and Anita and not to speak. I'll give you a chance to make any comments you'd like at the end of our discussion.

IV. Concluding Statement

Keith, my purpose in setting those limits was that I felt that Anita was seeking your approval. I wanted to have her speak directly to Linda and say what was on her mind without seeking any direction from you. I'm interested in hearing what you think about all this.

V. Guideline

Genogram

TECHNIQUE

Caring Days

I. *Source*

Based on Stuart, R. (1980). *Helping couples change: A social learning approach to marital therapy.* New York: Guilford Press.

II. *Brief Description*

Caring days is an exercise that enables a couple to tell each other the exact behavior each can exhibit to show that each cares for the other. The behavior must be specific, small, and done on a daily basis; it should not be a chore. Also, the behavior must not have been the cause of a recent conflict.

III. *Initial Statement*

Over the last few weeks I've heard you, Keith, express your concern that Linda doesn't have any time for you because of her involvement with Ruth. Linda, your concern has been that you and Keith talk only about Anita and the trouble she causes for the family. What I'd like you to do is make a list of ten behaviors that can finish the sentence "I feel loved when you . . ." (for example, "I feel loved when you hug me in the morning before I go to work"). Then I'd like you to put the list on your refrigerator. Next, I want you each to agree to do at least five of these items on a weekly basis and mark the date next to the item when you have done it.

IV. *Concluding Statement*

Linda, it's very easy to get so involved with the needs of the children and other responsibilities within the family that you lose touch with each other and your relationship as a couple. If you agree to do at least five of these items weekly, it will help strengthen the friendship and affection between you.

V. *Worksheet*

Caring days

TECHNIQUE

Challenging the Communication

I. Source
Based on Minuchin, S., Montalvo, B., Guerney, B., Rosman, B., & Schumer, F. (1976). *Families of the slums.* New York: Basic Books.

II. Brief Description
Frequently, communication within families is based on relationships rather than on content. Challenging the communication will help to change the rules of communication within the family. Each family member is asked to name a person to whom they will speak and demand that the person respond. This process helps people to use words to describe problems as well as solve them; it therefore increases the focus on content rather than relationship. The idea is to communicate cognitively rather than emotionally.

III. Initial Statement
Linda, you've expressed your anger about Anita's behavior and your disappointment that Keith doesn't seem to understand your feelings. Keith, you've been very clear about your belief that Linda is overreacting to Anita. You say that you don't even listen when Linda tells you how frustrated she is. You say that you tune her out when she demands that you comment or give her your opinion about the situation.

IV. Concluding Statement
We're using this technique to help Linda focus on a specific behavior and to encourage Keith to respond to her concern. Instead of Linda's making generalized complaints about Anita and Keith's tuning her out, focusing on content creates the opportunity to identify a specific problem and help you to work together to solve it.

V. Guideline
Communication

TECHNIQUE

Challenging the Structure

I. Source
Based on Minuchin, S., Montalvo, B., Guerney, B., Rosman, B., & Schumer, F. *Families of the slums.* New York: Basic Books.

II. Brief Description
This method challenges the structure of the family. First, the therapist identifies a pattern of interaction within the family. Then the family decides on one of the following options: to obey the existing pattern, to disobey it in an indirect way, to disobey it in a direct way, or to eliminate the pattern entirely.

III. Initial Statement
Linda, during our sessions you've complained about Anita and her rudeness toward you. Although Keith listens to your concern, he says Anita doesn't do these things in front of him, so it's hard for him to correct her after the fact. Therefore, I'm asking you, Linda, to confront Anita directly about her behavior. For example, you could say, "I get angry, Anita, when you don't answer me after I ask you a question."

IV. Concluding Statement
Linda, I understand you've been worried that if you correct Anita it might make the tension increase, and Keith is reluctant to get involved unless he sees the behavior firsthand. So Anita's negative behavior toward you, Linda, goes unchallenged. Speaking directly to Anita when the negative behavior occurs will interrupt the existing negative behavior and help prevent it from continuing.

V. Worksheet
Pathway

TECHNIQUE

Childhood Home

I. *Source*

Based on James, M., & Jongeward, D. *Born to win: Transactional analysis with gestalt experiments.* (1971). Philadelphia: Addison-Wesley.

II. *Brief Description*

This technique is useful for adults in a family who are experiencing difficulty with levels of recall about their childhood. This difficulty may prevent them from experiencing deeper levels of intimacy in the present. "Childhood Home" can help recover important memories.

III. *Initial Statement*

Linda and Keith, close your eyes. Imagine yourself back in the first home you can remember. Let the pictures emerge. Don't include what you think ought to be there, only what you see. What do you actually see? People? Furniture? Look around the room for details: colors, shapes, decorations. Now try to re-experience your other senses in relation to this home. What do you hear? Smell? Taste? Become aware of the people in your childhood home. Look at their faces, gestures, postures, clothes. How are they interacting? How do they interact with you? What roles are being played? What are your roles?

IV. *Concluding Statement*

I hope that it is becoming clear that our childhood experiences stay with us and are present all the time. It may take you more than one visit to recover these memories. You may have more than one home to visit. It is valuable for the whole family to gain insight into what happened in your earlier lives, Keith and Linda. We all carry issues from our childhood homes, but in your case you probably have issues from your first marriages as well.

V. *Worksheet*

Childhood memory

TECHNIQUE

Circular Interview

I. Source

Based on Fleuridas, C., Nelson, T. S., & Rosenthal, D. M. (1986). The evolution of circular questions: Training family therapists. *Journal of Marital and Family Therapy, 12*(2), 113–127.

II. Brief Description

The therapist asks questions of each family member in a logical order until a circle of all the members is completed. This procedure helps define the role the symptom is playing within the family. The circular interview gives each member a chance to share his or her own perspective and to integrate the others' views of the problem.

III. Initial Statement

To help us see what role the tension between Anita and Linda is playing in your family, I will ask each of you a few questions. I'll begin with Keith and go around the circle until I end with Mark. Answer from your own viewpoint, and listen carefully to one another.

IV. Concluding Statement

Now we can use this information to help each of you identify what has been said. I hope it also helps you begin to understand one another's views of the situation.

V. Guideline

Circular questions

TECHNIQUE

Circular Questions

I. Source
Based on Tomm, K. (1984). One perspective of the Milan systemic approach: Part II. Description of session format, interviewing style and interventions. *Journal of Marital and Family Therapy, 10,* 253–271.

II. Brief Description
Circular questions are used to assess the role of the presenting symptom on the family system. The therapist asks each person questions pertaining to problem definition, interactional sequences, classification, comparison, and intervention, in a logical sequence of present and past. (The guideline in Part Three gives examples.)

III. Initial Statement
I'm going to ask each of you some questions, so I can begin to understand how things are in your family. Let's start with Keith. What do you think Linda would say the problem is now?

IV. Concluding Statement
You have all been very helpful in answering my questions. I am beginning to understand how the Evans family works. Today, I have learned more about the role your presenting problem—Linda and Anita's relationship—has played in your family system. I am looking forward to discussing this with you. Together, we'll come up with some solutions.

V. Guideline
Circular questions

TECHNIQUE

Communication Game

I. *Source*

Based on Satir, V. (1983). *Conjoint family therapy: A guide to theory and technique.* Palo Alto, CA: Science & Behavior Books.

II. *Brief Description*

Communication games are a series of techniques that teach people to increase awareness and to be effective communicators. Based on the growth model, this series concretely shows individuals what happens when they do and do not look, touch, and speak in a congruent manner—the premise being that it's impossible for a person who has contact with the listener to send an incongruent message.

III. *Initial Statement*

We have been discussing how you talk about your needs and desires to one another. Rather than just talk about this, I would like to work with you on improving your communication skills. I will instruct you clearly on what to do at each step. Briefly, the steps include various verbal and nonverbal modes of communication: standing back to back and talking; turning face to face to look at each other without talking; looking and touching each other without talking; touching with your eyes closed and while talking; looking and talking without touching; and last, talking, touching, looking, and arguing with each other. We'll talk about each step as you try it, so you gain some insight into your communication. Let's get started.

IV. *Concluding Statement*

This last step showed that it is very difficult to send an angry, inconsistent, or inappropriate message to someone when you are talking, touching, and maintaining direct eye contact. Likewise, when a person is sending you a mixed message, he or she is probably out of touch with you.

V. *Worksheet*

Communication roadblocks

TECHNIQUE

Communication Stances

I. *Source*

Based on Satir, V., & Baldwin, M. (1983). *Satir step by step: A guide to creating change in families.* Palo Alto, CA: Science & Behavior Books.

II. *Brief Description*

Using communication stances, family members participate in a role-playing exercise by displaying the attitudes of the blamer, the placator, the distractor, the computer, and the congruent person. Afterward, family members discuss how being in that stance, as well as watching others in particular stances, affected them. This new awareness can help family members become more adept at communication and, as a result, learn to be themselves.

III. *Initial Statement*

Keith and Linda, let's experiment a little with how we communicate. There are at least four styles of communication, and each one has a physical position associated with it. The blamer can be thought of as one person shaking a finger at another while blaming and disagreeing with that person. The computer has a straight back and speaks logically, denying feeling. The placator agrees with the other and can be seen as kneeling, with the head bent up at an awkward angle. The distractor tries to change the subject; think of a person shaking his or her head. The congruent person is able to receive and process information accurately and has an open body position. I would like each of you to try talking to other family members, changing from one to another of these exaggerated physical positions with each person you talk to. We'll take ten minutes to do this. I would like you to observe the feelings that you experience in each position as you talk, as well as the feelings that come up for you as the other chooses a position.

IV. *Concluding Statement*

When we have a visual picture of how we see one another, most of us can begin to choose what we want to change.

V. *Guideline*

Stances

TECHNIQUE

Conflict Management

I. Source
Based on Stuart, R. (1980). *Helping couples change: A social learning approach to marital therapy.* New York: Guilford Press.

II. Brief Description
Couples who are able to communicate within specified roles are better able to prevent conflict. Several skills assist in limiting conflicts. One is to keep discussions in the here and now, instead of bringing up issues from the past.

III. Initial Statement
Keith and Linda, communication within families is very important. Many times this communication is blocked due to conflicts that arise around certain issues. I would like for each of you to discuss an issue you might have concerning the family. I do have one rule, though: when you are speaking, you must keep things in the present. What has happened in the past or what might happen in the future should not enter the discussion.

IV. Concluding Statement
This technique was designed to allow for discussion while keeping the conflicts between each other at a minimum. By speaking only about things that deal in the here and now, you were better able to keep focused on the issues at hand.

V. Guideline
Stances

TECHNIQUE

Contingency Contract

I. Source
Based on Brown, J., & Christensen, D. (1986). *Family therapy: Theory and practice.* Pacific Grove, CA: Brooks/Cole.

II. Brief Description
The contingency contract is a written agreement between parents and child that helps them devise a system for identifying their needs. The sequence of steps facilitates communication and sets up crucial interactions with family members to foster more successful parental management and understanding. The contingency contract helps each participant know what is expected of him or her and what may be gained in return.

III. Initial Statement
In order to help you understand more clearly what you each want from others and what you are each willing to offer, I want the whole family to write the answers to the questions on this paper. I will help you judge how appropriate the terms of the contract are.

IV. Concluding Statement
Keith and Linda, now that we have completed this contract, I hope you have a clearer idea of what you need from each other, what the costs are to each of you, and how to bargain and compromise more effectively. I think putting your ideas in writing has proved a more objective way of dealing with issues.

V. Worksheet
Simple contract

TECHNIQUE

Crediting

I. Source
Based on Boszormenyi-Nagy, I., & Framo, J. (Eds.). (1965). *Intensive family therapy*. New York: Harper & Row.

II. Brief Description
The therapist selects a family member, who then tells the family how he or she contributes to the family's well-being. The therapist typically begins with the underdog of the family, particularly a member triangled between two members who are in conflict.

III. Initial Statement
Keith Jr., you told us that you feel that no one cares about how much you help out around the house. I want you to tell your parents exactly all the things you do each week to make things at home run smoothly for them. I remember one of the things you said was that you babysit for the younger brother and sisters when your parents aren't home.

IV. Concluding Statement
I asked Keith Jr. to describe to us the ways he helps out at home because he feels that he does not receive credit for his help. He explained to us that he does not mind taking care of the younger children when asked to do so. It's just that he resents it, Linda, when you tell him he doesn't do his share of chores around the house. Keith Jr. listed jobs he does that he feels are important and a big help to you as parents. Sometimes people need to be recognized for a job well done; it makes them feel good, and it's important that they feel appreciated. Could you both add to Keith Jr.'s list some other things that he does to help you?

V. Worksheet
Time cable

TECHNIQUE

Dealing with Anger

I. *Source*
Based on Carter, L., & Minirth, F. (1993). *The anger workbook*. Nashville: Thomas Nelson Publishers.

II. *Brief Description*
In most conflict situations, anger plays a big role. To deal with it, a family needs to identify the source of anger for each of the members. The process involves, first, awareness; then, understanding; finally, action.

III. *Initial Statement*
Keith and Linda, I have noticed that lots of anger comes up in these sessions. Each of you seems to be angry about different things and different people. Today we are going to spend time examining what you are angry about and what the whole family wants to do about it. I have a worksheet to get you started.

IV. *Concluding Statement*
Just being aware of what you are angry about is not enough. You as a family need to choose what each of you want to do and how you can each help one another.

V. *Worksheet*
Anger

TECHNIQUE

Defining the Problem

I. *Source*
Based on Cormier, L. S., & Hackney, H. (1987). *The professional counselor: A process guide to helping.* Englewood Cliffs, NJ: Prentice-Hall.

II. *Brief Description*
To define the problem, each family member contributes to the definition without becoming defensive. The problem must be stated in behavioral language. If there is more than one problem, the most troublesome must be identified and made the target of counseling. Past attempts to solve the problem should be described in detail.

III. *Initial Statement*
So I can be effective in helping your family, it's important that we come up with a clear picture of the problem you're having. Dad thinks Mark and Kim are disrespectful, and they think Dad doesn't really care. Given these two different explanations, we can agree that the problem is the number of arguments. The family problem is not your attitudes—being disrespectful or overbearing. Instead, it is the frequency of your arguments. Linda, I know you are also concerned about Anita's problems at school, but the family has decided that the problem is the arguing. I know that you've put a lot of effort into solving this problem.

IV. *Concluding Statement*
We've agreed today that we should work on the problem of the frequent fights between the children and Keith. We will only be dealing with this one problem. We know the solutions you've tried already, so I won't repeat them.

V. *Worksheet*
Defining the problem

TECHNIQUE

Detriangling

I. Source
Bowen, M. (1966). The use of family theory in clinical practice. *Comprehensive Psychiatry, 7*(5), 345–374.

II. Brief Description
This technique is mastered when family members are able to listen to one another's views and feedback without becoming defensive or being drawn into an emotional battle. The result is an atmosphere of permissiveness, which allows for open conversation among family members.

III. Initial Statement
Keith, Linda, and Anita, I would like to work with the three of you for now. It seems to me, Keith, that there is a great deal of tension between your daughter and your wife. Anita feels that you are the only parent who listens to her. I would like both you and Linda to tell Anita that she may have the floor now to express whatever thoughts and feelings she has without fear of being punished or interrupted. Do you both agree? When Anita is finished speaking, I would like Keith to do the same thing while Anita and Linda listen. When Keith is through, Linda will have a chance to talk about what's on her mind while Keith and Anita listen to her.

IV. Concluding Statement
The reason I chose to work with the three of you alone was that I feel you each need to learn how to talk and listen to one another. To work problems out, you have to try to understand how each person involved is feeling. By listening to someone attentively, you are giving them your respect. That helps make discussions among the three of you less tense and easier to work through.

V. Guideline
Encouragement

TECHNIQUE

Empty Chair

I. Source
Based on Corey, G. (1991). *Theory and practice of counseling and psycho-therapy* (4th ed.). Pacific Grove, CA: Brooks/Cole.

II. Brief Description
The empty chair is a role-play technique for a client who is having difficulty expressing emotions. The empty chair represents another individual, or part of the client. The client plays all parts, so that he or she can experience an unresolved conflict more fully in the here and now, and begin the process of resolution.

III. Initial Statement
Keith, I want you to imagine that your father is sitting in this chair. Please tell him about your disappointments in him as a father. Express your feelings as his son. Live your disappointments, instead of analyzing them as an adult. When you're through, move to the other chair and reply as your father would have replied to you if you had actually had the opportunity to say these things to him.

IV. Concluding Statement
As you see, Keith, you were able to get rid of some anger and sadness that you had been holding inside for a long time. Perhaps, by playing your father's role, you gained a new perspective on how he may have felt. Your children may now have a better idea of the feelings you experienced in your childhood relationship with your father.

V. Guideline
Empty chair

TECHNIQUE

Enactment

I. *Source*
Based on Minuchin, S., & Fishman, H. C. (1981). *Family therapy techniques.* Cambridge, MA: Harvard University Press.

II. *Brief Description*
In this technique, the therapist constructs an interpersonal scenario during the session in which typical transactions between family members are played out. The transaction takes place within the session, in the here and now, and in relation to the therapist. The therapist can alter the enactment by increasing its intensity, prolonging its duration, and moving the family toward alternative ways of dealing with problems.

III. *Initial Statement*
Keith, I want a clear view of what happens when you have difficulty with Kim and Mark. I want you to imagine you are at home asking Mark and Kim to do a household chore. Mark and Kim, I want you to respond to your father as if you were at home.

IV. *Concluding Statement*
Through this enactment we individually have gained a clear picture of who does what and how each of you feels about following directions. Keith, I believe you heard these two for the first time.

V. *Guideline*
Role playing

TECHNIQUE

Encouraging

I. Source

Based on Crabb, L., & Allender, D. (1984). *Encouragement: The key to caring*. Grand Rapids, MI: Zondervan Publishing House.

II. Brief Description

The therapist helps to build up each family member by encouraging him or her to express feelings and to allow others to express theirs while getting closer to one another. The therapist encourages family members to take risks by sharing real feelings and to begin taking responsibility for their own behavior.

III. Initial Statement

I would like each of you to express your feelings about Mark's problem behavior. As each of you speaks, there should be no interruption from other family members. Before we begin focusing on Mark's problem, I would like each member to tell Mark in your own words that he is a valued member of this family, and give him an example of how he is important.

IV. Concluding Statement

It seems that each of you has been displeased, not only with Mark's behavior, but with one another's behavior as well. We all saw how difficult it was for Mark to identify what he actually wants and needs. No child of eight is really able to ask for the attention and hugs they need in a direct way. You can all feel better about yourselves by trying to figure out what you really want from the other person, and being unafraid to ask for it.

V. Guideline

Encouragement

TECHNIQUE

Encouraging a Response

I. *Source*
Based on Haley, J. (1973). *Uncommon therapy.* New York: Norton.

II. *Brief Description*
Encouraging a response by using frustration is an effective technique to deal with resistant clients who are unwilling to participate in the family session. In this situation, the therapist actually keeps the client from responding, which results in frustration and therefore, paradoxically, encourages the client to respond.

III. *Initial Statement*
Keith Jr., I noticed that you are shy and don't seem to want to participate here in our group work. I would like to respect that feeling and ask you not to respond to our discussion for the next ten minutes. I'll let you know when the ten minutes has passed.

IV. *Concluding Statement*
Keith Jr., the ten minutes is passed. I appreciate your respecting my request. Is there anything you would like to say at this time?

V. *Guideline*
Encouragement

TECHNIQUE

Expectations Game

I. Source
Based on Stevens, J. O. (1981). *Awareness: Exploring, experimenting, experiencing.* New York: Bantam.

II. Brief Description
One family member picks another as a partner. Each partner alternates telling the other their expectations for about five minutes. Then each is to summarize what they expect from each other, not interrupting to discuss or argue. Each will then express how he or she feels about these expectations. Next, the partners discuss their expectations in any way they desire. Finally, each partner tells the other how he or she does not live up to the other's expectations.

III. Initial Statement
Keith and Linda, in order to help you clearly understand what you expect from each other and your feelings about the other's expectations, I want you to alternate telling each other your expectations. After you have discussed them, I want you to summarize what you expect from each other, but please do not interrupt each other to discuss or argue. Just be sure that you understand each other. Next, express how each of you feels about these expectations. You might express which expectations are really important to you and which you are happy to meet. Then discuss them in any way you desire.

IV. Concluding Statement
I hope that you have begun to clarify your relationships and your demands on each other through this exercise. Ask yourself these questions: Did I try to evade my partner's expectations and try to impose my own? In what ways did we make honest, direct contact with each other? My hope is that you now have a way to continue the process outside this session.

V. Worksheet
Expectations

TECHNIQUE

Extinction

I. *Source*
Based on Granvold, D. (1994). *Cognitive and behavioral treatment: Methods and applications.* Pacific Grove, CA: Brooks/Cole.

II. *Brief Description*
Extinction is the process of eliminating an undesirable behavior through nonreinforcement of the target behavior. Consistency is important, because intermittent reinforcement will perpetuate the targeted behavior.

III. *Initial Statement*
Right now, Ruth's tantrums work for her, in that she gets your attention and usually ends up getting whatever she wants. Whenever you cater to her tantrums, you are actually reinforcing them; she knows they work. Keith and Linda, I'd like you to try a behavioral technique that I think may be an effective way to begin reducing the success of Ruth's tantrums. It involves consistently not reinforcing her tantrums so that they are eliminated. Whenever Ruth acts up and demands something she can't have, I want you first to say no and then to ignore her. Don't allow her to interrupt what you are doing. Don't negotiate with her.

IV. *Concluding Statement*
Keith and Linda, I know this change in your response will be frustrating at first because Ruth will continue to test you, but I think you will eventually notice a change in Ruth. She will begin to see that screaming and crying no longer gets her anywhere. Next week, we'll see how this process is working.

V. *Guideline*
Extinction

TECHNIQUE

Family Choreography

I. *Source*
Based on Papp, P. (1976). Family choreography. In P. Guerin (Ed.), *Family therapy: Theory and practice*. Gardner Press: New York.

II. *Brief Description*
This experiential technique originated from psychodrama. Family members are asked to position themselves in two ways. First, they arrange themselves to reflect how they see the family. Second, they position themselves to reflect how they would like to see the family. Members are asked to reenact a family scene, both as they see it in the present and as they would like to see it in the future.

III. *Initial Statement*
We have been exploring the issue of how little time Anita spends with the family, but we don't seem to be making any progress. I'm not sure I have a clear picture of what is going on at home. I would like to give each family member a chance to show me what the situation was like. Think about where everyone was when the argument began. Physically place each person in the position where he or she started, then move them around as the story unfolds. I would like you to now position each family member where you would like that person to be after the problem has been resolved. As you proceed, I'll be asking questions, so I can understand what is going on and how you are feeling. How about you going first, Anita?

IV. *Concluding Statement*
Anita, the words people say to one another usually become very predictable. Your family has learned how to use words to argue, deny, rationalize, accuse, defend, and cover up. We have introduced the element of surprise, and without words, your emotional behaviors had a chance to emerge more freely and clearly. Choreography provided us with a better understanding of the experience, and now we can map out the tasks that should be accomplished next.

V. *Guideline*
Psychodrama

TECHNIQUE

Family Council

I. Source
Based on Grunwald, B. B., & McAbee, H. V. (1985). *Guiding the family: Practical counseling techniques.* Muncie, IN: Accelerated Development.

II. Brief Description
Family council is a meeting of all the family members in one household to discuss a particular issue or problem. Each member states his or her opinion about the problem and what actions he or she would like to see occur to bring about a resolution. All viewpoints are taken into consideration as the family decides which direction is best.

III. Initial Statement
Keith and Linda, this week I want you to hold a family meeting to discuss one issue that your family thinks is important. You are the leaders, but each member should express his or her viewpoint and contribute to the decision-making process. You need to decide on a place and time for this meeting. I want this to become a weekly event, and being consistent about the day and time will help each member plan. I'll help you decide on an issue this week, to get you started.

IV. Concluding Statement
I want you to experience the power a family has to solve conflicts on its own using the family council. I understand that this idea may not be popular with Anita and Keith Jr., but I believe you will find it helpful in resolving family conflicts. I will give you a family minutes worksheet to bring back to our next session so that I can help you talk about your first family meeting.

V. Worksheet
Family minutes

TECHNIQUE

Family Drawings

I. Source
Based on Snider, M. (1992). *Process family therapy.* Boston: Allyn & Bacon.

II. Brief Description
Family members are asked to draw, individually or as a group, any or all of the following: anything they desire; a family drawing of all members of the family; an abstract family drawing; a drawing based on whatever results from scribbling with eyes closed. The drawing process provides valuable information on how the family interacts. The drawing itself can be seen as a metaphor for the individual in this interaction.

III. Initial Statement
I'd like everyone in the family to draw a picture for me. I want it to be one picture that you all work on together: you're free to draw whatever you wish. You don't have to be an artist. Here's a piece of paper and some markers. Go for it. You will have about ten minutes.

IV. Concluding Statement
This exercise allows me to see how your family works together. How the family chooses to finish the picture shows me how all of you work together on a project. I'd like each of you to tell me about this experience.

V. Materials
Clean paper or newsprint
Five pens or pencils
Five flat boards

TECHNIQUE

Family Lunch

I. *Source*

Based on Minuchin, S., Rosman, B., & Baker, L. (1978). *Psychosomatic families.* Cambridge, MA: Harvard University Press.

II. *Brief Description*

The family lunch was developed for families with an anorexic. In this technique, the therapist observes the interaction of the family members during lunch. Typically, a struggle takes place between the parents, who urge the anorexic to eat, and the child, who refuses. The goal of the session is to transform the issue of an anorexic client into the drama of a dysfunctional family.

III. *Initial Statement*

Linda, you have told me about your daughter's refusal to eat. I realize that you can't provide me with all the information I would need in order to help. So, I would like to invite you and the rest of your family to have lunch here with me. That way I can see exactly the kind of interaction that goes on around the table.

IV. *Concluding Statement*

Linda and Anita, a definite power struggle seems to be going on between the two of you. Linda, with your permission, I am going to take over Anita's eating program. Your job is to focus on the rest of the family for the next month.

V. *Worksheet*

Simple contract

TECHNIQUE

Family Reconstruction

I. Source
Based on Satir, V., & Baldwin, M. (1983). *Satir step by step: A guide to creating a change in families.* Palo Alto, CA: Science & Behavior Books.

II. Brief Description
Family reconstruction requires an individual to develop a map of the family, a history of the family, and a circle of influence. The therapist uses these tools to ask questions and develop scenes about the family's history, from the parents' meeting to the present, including the birth of the children into the family.

III. Initial Statement
Keith and Linda, for the next week, I would like you to develop a chronological history of your family, a map of your family, and a circle of influence. Let me tell you about each of these. First, the history begins as far back as your parents' meeting and continues to the present, giving dates, events, who was there, and the setting. Next, develop a map of your family consisting of at least three generations—that would include you, your parents' generation, and your grandparents' generation. Finally, I need a circle of influence, which is a circle with you at the center and a spoke going out to each significant person in your life. The thicker the spoke, the more important that person is to you. Do you have any questions? You can get the kids to help you with this if you like.

IV. Concluding Statement
This assignment is intended to help you discover yourselves and your parents as people, and to help the family know their history. We might not be able to go over all of this next week, but we will start.

V. Guideline
Genogram

TECHNIQUE

Family Secrets

I. Source
Based on Ackerman, N. (1958). *The psychodynamics of family life: Diagnosis and treatment of family relationships.* New York: Basic Books.

II. Brief Description
When an issue arises that a family does not want to talk about, that issue is usually significant. The family's silence itself communicates something. The therapist calls attention to the silence and discusses it using a technique called family secrets.

III. Initial Statement
I would like to talk about what this silence is doing or not doing for the family. Keith, why do you think this subject brings silence upon the family? What do you think the silence is saying?

IV. Concluding Statement
I hope this has helped you look at and become aware of why you are silent about this issue. We need to discover what each of your concerns are if the silent issue surfaces. Being silent is not going to resolve the issue.

V. Worksheet
Nonverbal cue

TECHNIQUE

Fighting Fair

I. Source

Based on Stuart, R. (1980). *Helping couples change: A social learning approach to marital therapy.* New York: Guilford Press.

II. Brief Description

Fighting fair teaches families how to communicate better by introducing certain rules to apply when arguments come up. When anger is triggered in the relationship, it is important to keep the discussion confined to the present, rather than expanding to a related incidents or issues from the past. Insults and attacks on a mate's vulnerable areas, such as weight or job status, only lead to intensified feelings of hurt and anger. Other rules include no name-calling; no personalizing; no teasing; and no bossing. All add up to methods to make arguments more fair.

III. Initial Statement

Keith and Linda, it seems that the members of this family have a need to shout at one another and argue much of the time. This need shows great strength of character. Fighting for what you think is right is an important family value. But it has its price. Perhaps we can find some way to confine the fighting to a specific time of day, so that it will cost less and still accomplish the useful ends you achieve by fighting. I recommend waiting at least a half-hour after dinner, so you can digest your meal. Each family member can keep a journal so that you fight about everything that comes up during your day.

IV. Worksheet

Obstacles analysis

TECHNIQUE

Focus on Strengths

I. *Source*

Based on Ackerman, N. (1958). *The psychodynamics of family life: Diagnosis and treatment of family relationships.* New York: Basic Books.

II. *Brief Description*

The therapist takes an active role in reflecting the healthy aspects of a family's functioning. Families in difficulty may not be able to see the positive aspects of their relationships. They may need to rely on the therapist to develop communication and empathy among family members, to clarify and point out coping mechanisms, to support and nurture the family, and to teach and model healthy family functioning.

III. *Initial Statement*

Keith and Linda, when I hear you talk about the ways you have tried to include all your children in your plans, it's clear to me that you are united in your intent to make this family run smoothly. I think that your commitment to working out the problems in this family is a real strength.

IV. *Concluding Statement*

Together we can use the commitment you have developed to sort out the conflicts you and your children are having now.

V. *Guideline*

Group leadership skills

TECHNIQUE

Formula Task

I. Source

Based on O'Hanlon, W. H., & Weiner-Davis, M. (1989). *In search of solutions: A new direction in psychotherapy.* New York: Norton.

II. Brief Description

At the end of the first session with a family, the therapist asks family members to go home and observe a particular part of their lives. Relationships, family life, and marriage are examined to identify the positive qualities that family members want to maintain. In the next therapy session, the family is to describe these positive qualities.

III. Initial Statement

Linda, before our next session, I want you to take notice of the things that go on in your family that you really like and that you want to continue to characterize your family in the future. During our next session, I want you to report to me and your family all the things you noticed that you liked and that you want to continue.

IV. Concluding Statement

The purpose of this assignment is to have you uncover some things that are working for your family. Many of these things may surprise you, because you never stopped to notice them before. While I told only you, Linda, to identify good things, I believe that it is important for each family member to do the same thing. Recognizing positive aspects of family life is just as important as identifying negative aspects. You may find this perspective useful in the future when resolving your family's issues and concerns.

V. Worksheet

Observation

TECHNIQUE

Genogram

I. Source

Based on McGoldrick, M., & Gerson, R. (1985). *Genograms in family assessment.* New York: Norton.

II. Brief Description

A genogram is a diagram of a family's relationship in the form of a genetic tree including at least three generations, tracing the father's and the mother's families of origin through members of the current family. Although used primarily as an information-gathering tool, the genogram can also be used to help build rapport between client and therapist, to provoke discussion on issues originating in the family of origin, and to indicate certain themes that run through a family. The genogram can also provide clues to problems, help children to learn more about their parents, help to cool down a heated interaction, and slow down a session that is proceeding too quickly.

III. Initial Statement

What are we going to do now is an exercise that involves gathering some background information from each of you. This will help me to become better acquainted with you. I am going to have each of you answer some questions while I construct the Evans family tree. It will consist of three generations, including the two in this room and your parents, Keith and Linda. I'll need the names of the family members. We'll make some notes on their important life events. We'll also take a look at the relationships among members of the immediate family.

IV. Concluding Statement

As you see, while mapping out your family tree you discovered many new things about one another. Many aspects of relationships in your families of origin are similar to aspects of your present family's relationships. I hope making your family tree has given all of you a new perspective with which to view one another.

V. Guideline

Genogram

TECHNIQUE

Harmony among Parts

I. Source
Based on Ackerman, N. (1958). *The psychodynamics of family life: Diagnosis and treatment of family relationships.* New York: Basic Books.

II. Brief Description
Harmony among parts refers to the coordination of family members in expressing themselves and uniting in actions. Each member is responsible for working with the others to create a smoothly running family machine.

III. Initial Statement
From what I have heard in our sessions, there is a great deal of uncertainty about the expected role of each member of this family. I'd like to make a list of the Evans family qualities. Keith and Linda, I'd like you each to give one characteristic that you believe you should have in order to be a good parent, and one characteristic that you believe is necessary for a good son or daughter to have. While you are thinking about your answer, I want you to keep in mind what you think your children desire from you; kids, I want you to think about what your parents would want you to say.

IV. Concluding Statement
My goal is for the children to say, "Yeah, I want a mom and a dad like that," and for you, Linda and Keith, to have the same kind of response to the children's answers. I believe it benefits the entire family for each member to agree on his or her role in the family unit and to understand one another.

V. Worksheet
Problem solving

TECHNIQUE

Homework

I. Source
Based on Haley, J. (1976). *Problem-solving therapy: New strategies for effective family therapy.* New York: Harper Colophon Books.

II. Brief Description
A homework assignment is a task the therapist may give a family at the end of a session. The task may be simple or complex. When given an assignment to follow, the family remains involved with the therapist between sessions. The assignment is usually global in nature, changing how a family interacts as opposed to troubleshooting. Results of the homework assignment are discussed during the next session.

III. Initial Statement
Between now and our session next week, I would like each of you to do a task. I sense that you each blame someone else for your feeling bad. During this week I want you to stop blaming others for your bad feelings. Instead, I want you to make an "I" statement. Linda, when you feel angry about something, say "I feel angry," instead of "You make me mad." Keith, you say "I feel guilty," instead of "You make me feel guilty." The children should follow your example.

IV. Concluding Statement
Using "I" statements allows you each to take ownership of your feelings. I hope you will be reminded throughout the week about what you have learned today. Next week I will check in to see how well the assignment worked out.

V. Worksheet
Time cable

TECHNIQUE

Homework Prescriptions

I. *Source*
Based on Russell, C. S., Anderson, S. A., Atilano, R. B., Jurich, A. P., & Bergen, L. P. (1984). Intervention strategies: Predicting family therapy outcome. *Journal of Marital and Family Therapy, 10,* 3, 241–251.

II. *Brief Description*
Tasks that deal with the restructuring of family interaction should be assigned to be done at home. Changing the boundary within a system helps to facilitate better communication and better understanding. The task is a prescription given to solve a specific problem within the system, much as an antibiotic is given for an infection.

III. *Initial Statement*
Keith, you say it shouldn't be Keith Jr.'s job to help in the kitchen, because he's a boy and that's not a man's work. You think Anita should do the kitchen chores, but she has an evening job and has to leave for work right after dinner. Anita has offered to cut the grass, if you show her how, in exchange for not doing kitchen chores. Linda, you don't think it's a problem for Keith Jr. to help you or for Anita to help Keith. You are angry at Keith because he's being chauvinistic and unreasonable. You don't think he's setting a good example as a parent, and you need some help around the house. Therefore, I am suggesting that you follow the plan suggested by Linda and Anita: Keith Jr. helps Linda with kitchen chores, and Keith shows Anita how to cut the grass.

IV. *Concluding Statement*
Keith, maybe teaching Anita how to do yard work will allow you to get to know your daughter better. It is important to acknowledge that in a family like yours, where everyone is expected to help out, it doesn't really matter who does what as long as everything that needs to be done is done.

V. *Worksheet*
Relabeling

TECHNIQUE

Humor Applied

I. Source
Based on Napier, R. W., & Gershenfeld, M. K. (1987). *Groups: Theory and experience*. Boston: Houghton Mifflin.

II. Brief Description
Families often avoid humor when dealing with life's struggles. But looking at the absurdity of a situation or exaggerating it to gigantic proportions can lead to self-realization and insight. Ironic humor that evolves from distortions in reality can give us perspectives into our own self-deceptions.

III. Initial Statement
Keith and Linda, have you ever read "Life in the USA" in *Reader's Digest*? I want you to bring more humor into your family. The best place to start is with what you already know. I want you to think of funny stories about family events or things the children have said and done. Humor plays an important part in a healthy family, and I believe the family needs a joke book to record the funny things that happen.

IV. Concluding Statement
Once you have collected funny events in your family joke book, you can use this as a resource in times of tension, anxiety, or conflict. The more you write in and work on your joke book, the more useful it will be to your family.

V. Guideline
Humor

TECHNIQUE

"I" Statements

I. Source

Based on Wile, D. B. (1981). *Couples therapy: A nontraditional approach.* New York: John Wiley.

II. Brief Description

The therapist can model good communication skills and teach or train family members in effective communication. A technique for improving a family's communication skills involves teaching the members to use "I" statements rather than accusatory statements. "I" statements begin with phrases such as "I think" or "I feel," as opposed to such phrases as "You make me feel" or "It is so hard." This rephrasing changes not only the tone of the statement, but also makes it less likely that the statement will offend the other person.

III. Initial Statement

You have talked about things that other people say or do that upset you. Linda, while talking about work and being a mother of five, you've said, "It is hard." What I would like you to do now is take those same words and start them with "I." Linda, you could say, "I find working and being a mother of five difficult." Take responsibility for the things you say, think, and feel. Speaking this way, you will come across to another person as less judgmental. Others will be more open to your thoughts and feelings if you take responsibility.

IV. Concluding Statement

If you each own the statements you make, you will hear others' words and speak less defensively. It is very hard to argue without putting down the other person's feelings. When hearing such statements from another, make sure you don't tell the other person he or she shouldn't feel that way. Instead, listen to the person's reasons for voicing those feelings.

V. Worksheet

Communication roadblocks

VI. Guidelines

Communication
Listening

TECHNIQUE

Joining

I. Source
Based on Minuchin, S., & Fishman, H. C. (1981). *Family therapy techniques.* Cambridge, MA: Harvard University Press.

II. Brief Description
Joining involves the therapist's attempt to make a connection with each family member. It can be accomplished through imitation of affect and body language, or by accurately interpreting the content and feeling of a statement, as well as by creating a comfortable climate and discussing commonalities. Often joining can be achieved through self-disclosure, mirroring, or simply finding a common link.

III. Initial Statement
Keith and Linda, I can see why you feel frustrated when you get home from work and have to fight with the kids. Working as much as you do requires a lot of energy. When you get home, you're tired and don't feel like settling the latest family feud. I know how I feel when I get home at night and find that my day isn't over yet. I feel like I can't win either. Getting help from family members can bring relief.

IV. Concluding Statement
Now that our first session is over I feel I've had a good chance to learn a bit about each of you. As we continue to meet, I believe we will feel comfortable with one another and freely share our thoughts and ideas.

V. Guideline
Self-disclosure

TECHNIQUE

Live History

I. Source
Based on Ackerman, N. (1958). *The psychodynamics of family life: Diagnosis and treatment of family relationships.* New York: Basic Books.

II. Brief Description
As family members interrelate and patterns emerge, vital information is provided about experiences that occurred in the past. Family members also display how the past continues to be evident in the present structure and functioning of the family. Through observation, a therapist can learn about a family's past and how it influences the family in the present.

III. Initial Statement
Keith and Linda, by listening to you tell your stories and watching the way you relate to each other and to your children, I can see how your past marriages are influencing your present one. You have combined your past experiences into your current life, each bringing different qualities that merge into your relationship.

IV. Concluding Statement
By gathering information about your lives, I can better understand your past ways of being. That helps me see why you are the way you are and allows me to show you how your past influences your present. Resolving your current problems may be easier if we all understand how you have functioned in the past.

V. Worksheet
Marriage model

TECHNIQUE

Logical and Natural Consequences

I. *Source*
Based on Grunwald, B. B., & McAbee, H. V. (1985). *Guiding the family: Practical counseling techniques.* Muncie, IN: Accelerated Development.

II. *Brief Description*
Using logical and natural consequences is one way to teach children responsibility for their choices. Parents remain unemotional, neither arguing nor criticizing their children for misbehavior. For example, a child who has spent his allowance by the second day of the week is calmly told that he may not have an advance when the ice cream truck appears, but he may purchase ice cream next week if he saves his next allowance.

III. *Initial Statement*
Linda, you have told me how upset you get when Anita is continually late for dinner. This week, if Anita is late, try using logical consequences. Instead of yelling at her about how hard you worked to make a nice dinner or how disruptive it is to the family when she comes in late, simply remove her plate and utensils from the table when you sit down to eat, if she is not there. When she comes in, calmly tell her it's unfortunate that she could not be here to share the meal with the family, and you look forward to having her with you the next night.

IV. *Concluding Statement*
It may be difficult at first to remain calm, Linda, but if Anita understands that you are serious that everyone has to be on time for dinner and that you really want her to be at the table with the family, she will see she is not winning anything by being late.

V. *Guideline*
Discipline

TECHNIQUE

Looking

I. Source

Based on Barker, R. (1984). *Treating couples in crisis.* New York: Free Press.

II. Brief Description

A couple in crisis often stop looking at each other—what they see has become routine, programmed or choreographed. The therapist asks each partner to spend ten minutes looking at the other with no verbal or physical contact. Partners are not asked to stare, but rather to look at all parts of each other from many different angles, distances, and positions. The assignment literally asks each partner to observe the other from a different viewpoint.

III. Initial Statement

Keith and Linda, it seems that the two of you are so used to each other that you have completely stopped looking at each other. I would like you to try an exercise that will help you develop a new way of looking at each other. You may not talk to or touch each other, but feel free to move around and really look at each other from any distance or any angle that you please.

IV. Concluding Statement

In our busy day-to-day life, it's rare that we really spend time just looking at the people we are close to. Now that you have spent ten minutes looking at your partner, did you notice anything new or have any particular feelings about this person you married? How did it feel to be looked at so intently?

V. Worksheet

Nonverbal cues

TECHNIQUE

Marital Schism

I. *Source*
Based on Weiss, R. (1975). *Marital separation*. New York: Basic Books.

II. *Brief Description*
In marital schism, each parent is preoccupied with his or her own problems. The role that each parent takes in the family is not compatible with the other person's role. The result is that each parent begins to undermine the other's worth, and the parents end up competing for the children's loyalty, affection, sympathy, and support. Neither parent values or respects the other, and neither wants the children to grow up like the other parent. The parents often threaten to divorce or separate.

III. *Initial Statement*
Keith and Linda, I would like to do something a bit different to change the pace. I want each of you to take a puzzle box, sit in a separate corner of the room, and try as quickly as possible to get your puzzle together. Do not talk or communicate with each other at all. You may have any of your children help you complete the puzzle. The goal is to see who completes the puzzle first.

IV. *Concluding Statement*
OK, it's time to stop. For the next few minutes I want to talk about what was happening. You found that you could not complete your puzzle because each of you had pieces that the other person needed. You found it necessary to use the children to get the pieces that you needed to reach your goal. Sometimes the children cooperated with you; sometimes they didn't. Eventually they were forced to choose sides. In many ways your marriage is similar. Let's talk about that now.

V. *Worksheet*
Defining the problem

TECHNIQUE

Marital Stalemate

I. Source
Based on Selvini Palazzoli, M., Cirillo, S., Selvini, M., & Sorrentino, A. M. (1989). *Family games: General models of psychiatric processes in the family.* New York: Norton.

II. Brief Description
Often, one spouse has an intense fear about his or her partner. This fear could cause a stalemate in the relationship. If the therapist shares a hypothesis about this fear, the couple must address it by either confirming or denying it. Putting these feelings on the table will reduce the intensity of the fear.

III. Initial Statement
Keith and Linda, I believe we have something to talk about. I believe Linda has a fear so deep that it is greatly affecting your relationship. After talking to you these past several weeks, it has become clear to me that Linda fears you will not respect her and will speak unkindly to her as you do about your ex-wife. Her fear has made her wary of making mistakes with your children, and it underlies much of the difficulty she is having with Anita. Linda, does this sound right to you?

IV. Concluding Statement
We have talked about Linda's fear as I saw it. From our discussion, it seems I was correct. Linda is afraid of doing wrong in your eyes, but talking about her fear has clearly lessened it. I hope you will continue to communicate your deepest feelings with each other.

V. Worksheet
Marriage model

TECHNIQUE

Metaphor

I. Source
Based on Haley, J. (1986). *Uncommon therapy.* New York: Norton.

II. Brief Description
A metaphor is an effective way to help the family approach a difficult topic by discussing something that represents it. A therapist can make effective use of metaphors, slogans, and proverbs that relate to the family's day-to-day experience, especially when a person resists directives.

III. Initial Statement
(Linda and Keith are conflicted about their sexual relations but would rather not talk about the topic directly, so the therapist chooses to approach it metaphorically.) Linda and Keith, when you have dinner without the children, I know that you, Linda, enjoy having appetizers before dinner, while you, Keith, prefer to dive right into the meat and potatoes. I want the two of you to arrange a pleasant dinner on a particular evening that is satisfactory to both of you, when the children can sleep over at a relative's house.

IV. Concluding Statement
Each of you has a responsibility to the other to enjoy the evening.

V. Worksheet
Monitoring

TECHNIQUE

Monitoring

I. Source
Based on Lange, A., & Hart, D. (1983). *Directive family therapy.* New York: Brunner/Mazel.

II. Brief Description
Clients often complain about one another's behavior. These complaints are usually vague, such as "He never listens," or "She makes me feel unimportant." One way for them to get a clearer understanding of what they want or what irritates them is to write down everything they find irritating about the other person as it happens. This list should include things that the other does wrong as well as things the other fails to do.

III. Initial Statement
You've both talked about things the other one does or doesn't do that bother you. For example, Keith, you've said that you want Linda to listen to you more. Linda, you've said that you want Keith to take on more responsibility around the house. What I'd like for the two of you to do during the next week is to write down what you want from each other when a problem comes up—including things the other does that annoy you as well as things your partner fails to do. I'd like you to write exactly what it was you wanted or what irritated you, the date, the time, a very brief description, and how you felt. Don't say anything to each other; just write it down.

IV. Concluding Statement
If you have a clearer understanding of what you want from each other, you will be in a better position to ask for it clearly. By looking at how you feel about things your partner does that really get to you, you can begin to talk to each other about how you are affected by each other's actions.

V. Worksheet
Journal format

TECHNIQUE

Motivation

I. Source
Based on Boszormenyi-Nagy, I., with Krasner, B. R. (1986). *Between give and take: A clinical guide to contextual therapy.* New York: Brunner/Mazel.

II. Brief Description
This is a technique to motivate a person to take action. The therapist encourages clients to replace mutual blame with mutual accountability. Then family members are asked what action can be taken to improve their circumstances or make life better for themselves or the family.

III. Initial Statement
Linda, you've expressed your anger about Anita's ignoring you when you ask her questions. And Anita has said that she feels you're prying into areas of her life where she thinks she should have privacy. I would like the two of you to talk with each other about what Linda feels she needs to know as a parent and what Anita feels invades her privacy as a young lady. I would like the two of you to make a list of three things that Anita will agree to discuss or answer questions about with Linda and three things that Linda will agree not to ask Anita about because they are private.

IV. Concluding Statement
I want to help each of you to have a greater understanding of the other's needs and point of view. I hope also to help move you beyond the status quo of Linda's asking questions and Anita's ignoring her. Agreeing on even a few items that are open for discussion is a first step toward improving your current interaction.

V. Worksheet
Conflict resolution

TECHNIQUE

Multidirected Partiality

I. Source
Based on Boszormenyi-Nagy, I. (1966). From family therapy to a psychology of relationships: Fictions of the individual and fictions of the family. *Comprehensive Psychiatry, 7*(5), 408–423.

II. Brief Description
The therapist's goal is to be empathic with each member and understand each member's viewpoint. The therapist also attempts to uncover loyalties that may be hidden, thus increasing awareness of the entire family system.

III. Initial Statement
Keith and Linda, empathy is the ability to participate in another's feelings or ideas. Being part of a family often causes the members to become stuck in their own viewpoints or attitudes. The family benefits when one member begins to explore another's viewpoint and understand his or her perspective or feelings. For the next ten minutes, we are going to learn how to feel what someone else may be experiencing. I'll begin with Keith Jr. Watch how I begin to express what I think Keith Jr.'s feelings and thoughts about being here are. Keith Jr. will then tell me what he thinks my feelings or thoughts are. We will take turns practicing today.

IV. Concluding Statement
Understanding how another person feels or what he or she thinks about an interaction can open up communications and develop a healthy family. Empathy validates people, so that they feel that they count and belong to the family. I want you to use this technique twice this next week and to write down the results in a journal, so we can talk about your experiences next session.

V. Worksheet
Journal format

TECHNIQUE

Negotiated Quiet Time

I. Source
Based on Alexander, J., & Parsons, B. V. (1982). *Functional family therapy.* Pacific Grove, CA: Brooks/Cole.

II. Brief Description
Negotiated quiet time involves giving family members the opportunity for separation as well as closeness. Designed for use with working single parents, the technique has the parent negotiate for thirty minutes of private time, after which each child receives undivided parental attention.

III. Initial Statement
Linda, you've said that because you get home from work just before the children get off the school bus, you feel like you don't have a moment to catch your breath. The children are all after you at once, wanting to tell you about their day and asking for your help with their assignments. I'd like you to make a deal with them. If they'll give you half an hour of peace and quiet, you'll spend time alone with each of them afterward talking, helping with homework, or whatever. Part of the deal will involve working out a schedule, so each child knows when he or she will have a turn.

IV. Concluding Statement
Linda, it's good for you to take care of yourself and to remind yourself that you're a person as well as a mother. And your children can feel good about being on their own for those thirty minutes. When you do come together, you'll be relaxed and ready for some quality time.

V. Worksheet
Simple contract

TECHNIQUE

Negotiation

I. Source
Based on Patterson, G. (1975). *Professional guide for families living with children.* Champaign, IL: Research Press.

II. Brief Description
This technique fosters communication and problem solving through discussion of the problem as it arises and before it is blown out of proportion. A time and place is mutually selected for discussion with the partner. The partner shares the problem and accompanying feelings. The other partner listens and paraphrases what the first partner said. The second part of the process involves meeting again to negotiate behaviors more acceptable to each partner. The partners then sign a written contract.

III. Initial Statement
Keith and Linda, I know how frustrated you both become when problems get out of control. When one of you feels a problem is arising, I want you to negotiate a mutually agreed-upon time and place to tell the other what's wrong and how you feel about it. The other partner is to listen and paraphrase back what he or she hears. When you reach a clear understanding, you will agree to a later meeting time when you will define positive behaviors you would like to see in each other. Record any negative comments and finish the discussion at the agreed-upon time. Begin with the first item on the list and negotiate to exchange certain behaviors for others. Then, together agree on positive or negative consequences that will follow if the behavior is demonstrated. You should both sign this agreement as a written contract to show your mutual support for it.

IV. Concluding Statement
I feel that you both have good insights into what satisfies you. I am sure you will see over time how you can apply these insights.

V. Worksheet
Simple contract

TECHNIQUE

Ordeals

I. Source
Based on Haley, J. (1984). *Ordeal therapy: Unusual ways of changing behavior.* San Francisco: Jossey-Bass.

II. Brief Description
The therapist assigns family members a task. The objective of the task is to replace the family's problem with something more negative. The assigned task, however, is usually something that family members would not want to do and is more intense than the existing problem. If family members are experiencing tension when together for a short period of time, extend the period of time to make their time together an ordeal.

III. Initial Statement
Linda and Anita, I have noticed the amount of tension between you. I want the two of you to set aside an hour each day to do something fun or relaxing together. When you feel things are starting to get tense, drop what you are doing and take an hour for the activity. We will spend the next half-hour deciding what the activity will be.

IV. Concluding Statement
By taking the time to enjoy each other's company, the two of you will lessen the tension between you and replace it with a more positive interaction. You may not get anything done, but just try it for the next week.

V. Worksheet
Problem solving

TECHNIQUE

Paradoxical Double Bind

I. Source
Based on Palazzoli, M., Boscolo, L., Cecchin, G., & Prata, G. (1978). *Paradox and counter paradox*. New York: Jason Aronson.

II. Brief Description
People in a double bind situation are "damned if they do and damned if they don't." In a therapeutic double bind people are "changed if they do and changed if they don't." One type of double bind involves prescribing the symptom. If the person complies, the symptom is no longer involuntary and a degree of control is introduced. If the person does not comply (and so does not display the symptom), change has also occurred.

III. Initial Statement
Keith, your throwing dirty clothes on the bedroom floor has caused many arguments with Linda. Apart from these arguments, the two of you have very little to say to each other. For the time being, Keith, I would like you to continue throwing your clothes on the floor. Linda, I encourage you to stand your ground and continue to get upset about it. As a matter of fact, I would like you to make a point of having this argument more often. I think the time you and your wife spend together is very important. If it weren't for the dirty laundry, how would you stay in touch?

IV. Concluding Statement
I believe that by doing what we discussed earlier, things will get better. Since you've been arguing over clothes for years now, I don't imagine you will have any trouble continuing to do so, or even arguing more often. Just keep doing what you've been doing.

V. Worksheet
Johari window

TECHNIQUE

Paradoxical Interventions

I. Source
Based on Fisch, R., Weakland, J. H., & Segal, L. (1982). *The tactics of change: Doing therapy briefly.* San Francisco: Jossey-Bass.

II. Brief Description
With this technique the therapist recommends that clients try the opposite of solutions they have already tried; the technique is thus similar to reverse psychology. Paradoxical intervention aims only at behavior change and not at insight. For example, when a client is avoiding an activity out of fear of failure, the very avoidance becomes an underlying problem. The client comes in to be relieved of the fear of failure, but the paradoxical intervention aims at breaking the pattern of avoidance that holds the fear in place and magnifies it. In a paradoxical intervention, the client would be asked to perform the activity with failure as the goal.

III. Initial Statement
Linda, both you and Keith agree that your need to have the house neat and clean all the time is creating a lot of stress in the family. I see it as a sign of how much you care about your house. What I'd suggest is that for one week, until we meet next, you clean only when no one else is home. The rest of the family members can make a real mess, to give Linda something to clean. Linda, every time the last person leaves, jump up from whatever you are doing and clean for as long as you are alone. Do it every time you are alone in the house.

IV. Concluding Statement
Sometimes a behavior may seem like the problem, but the real problem arises when the behavior is restricted. I think you all can see how unfair the session was for Linda this week. How can we improve this situation?

V. Worksheet
Simple contract

TECHNIQUE

Paradoxical Prescription

I. *Source*
Based on Brown, J., & Christensen, D. (1986). *Family therapy: Theory and practice.* Pacific Grove, CA: Brooks/Cole.

II. *Brief Description*
Some couples may be resistant to therapy or any help that is offered. In such a case, a paradoxical prescription may be given in the form of a homework assignment. The therapist wants the couple to resist the assignment so that they will move toward improvement.

III. *Initial Statement*
Linda, you are concerned about the arguing among family members. You feel arguments arise when Keith is under pressure at work and comes home tense. He begins to yell and is not tolerant of the children. Every day, for the next week, when Keith gets home, he will yell at the children for one hour. If Keith is less tolerant with the children, it will help him become more and more relaxed. The children will understand. They're good for unloading frustration on and helping one to forget about problems.

IV. *Concluding Statement*
Keith has been under pressure at work for a long time. I do not want him to change his pattern; I actually want him to lower his tolerance level for the children in order to become relaxed. Let's follow this path for a week. Remember, the children will understand. This is a good way to release tension and has worked in the past.

V. *Worksheet*
Anger

TECHNIQUE

Parallel Examples

I. Source
Based on King, M., Novik, L., & Citrenbaum, C. (1983). *Irresistible communication: Creative skills for the health professional.* Philadelphia: W. B. Saunders.

II. Brief Description
With parallel examples, the therapist uses examples of how an individual coped with a problem in the past in order to help the same individual cope with a problem in the present. Ideally, a therapist looks for an experience in the past that is similar to the current situation. Reminding people how they overcame obstacles or simply how to enjoy life can be very empowering and help them get in touch with their resources.

III. Initial Statement
Keith and Linda, I'd like you to think back to when you were in grade school and were learning how to add and subtract. Remember how difficult it seemed? But you enjoyed it, and you even survived geometry, algebra, and calculus. Of course, math is different from marriage, but the point is that you both have shown you can do well by working hard for something that means a lot to you.

IV. Concluding Statement
At one time, each of you struggled and stumbled as you learned how to read and write. Now you don't even have to think about it—it's automatic. You've learned how to speak, and although it's been difficult lately, you can learn to speak to one another. It may be hard work at first, but eventually it will become second nature.

V. Worksheet
Time cable

TECHNIQUE

Past Successes

I. Source
Based on de Shazer, S. (1982). *Patterns of brief family therapy: An ecosystem approach.* New York: Guilford Press.

II. Brief Description
In this technique, the therapist congratulates and gives positive feedback for any successful resolution of past problems, but does not let past solutions influence the present situation. The therapist must acknowledge that if the past resolution had been the best one, the family would have solved the present problem.

III. Initial Statement
Linda, how you have dealt with similar situations in the past obviously has some bearing on what is going on today. What worked then may have been a simple solution to a complex problem, but that solution is no longer working. It's OK to bring up these past successes, but it's important to treat the new situation separately and not to rely on old ways of fixing a new problem. We want to come up with new ways to solve the present problem.

IV. Concluding Statement
We should be proud of and learn from past successes, but we cannot allow them to cloud our judgment in new situations. If a past solution really were the best one, then this new problem would not have come up.

V. Worksheet
Problem solving

TECHNIQUE

Person to Person

I. Source
Based on Piercy, F., Sprenkle, D., et al. (1986). *Family therapy source book.* New York: Guilford Press.

II. Brief Description
The goal of this technique is to direct family members to focus on themselves. This technique is particularly helpful with couples. The therapist joins with each partner in turn and encourages each to discuss several aspects of him- or herself in the presence of the other person. This process allows both clients to define their unique identities within the partnership.

III. Initial Statement
Keith and Linda, I would like to try something with each of you. I want each of you to tell me as many things as you can about yourself, such as your favorite movie, your hobbies, or your most embarrassing moment. Tell me about anything you feel is special or different about yourself. You can be as serious or as silly as you wish. Linda, I would like to begin with you. When you are finished, Keith will have his turn. Be sure to listen to each other.

IV. Concluding Statement
I asked each of you to do this activity because sometimes people tend to feel they are no longer their own person once they are married. It's also fun to learn interesting things about your spouse that you may not have known before you came here. This activity helps both of you to remember things about yourselves that make you special, as well as to see what's special and different about your spouse.

V. Guideline
Encouragement

TECHNIQUE

Photos

I. Source

Based on Sherman, R., & Fredman, N. (1986). *Handbook of structured techniques in marriage and family therapy.* New York: Brunner/Mazel.

II. Brief Description

A therapist can observe many important behaviors by asking a family to bring in photographs. Which pictures are shown first and last, who in the family was left out, how quickly or slowly the photos are shown, how much interest or anxiety is aroused, and how much joking or laughing accompanies the presentation may provide the therapist with information about the family system. Photographs can be reviewed for alignments, splits, and boundaries and also for customs, traditions, and special times the family has spent together.

III. Initial Statement

I would like each of you to bring in three photographs next week that say something important about your family. Each person will have up to ten minutes to talk about the photos. We will be talking about why you chose the pictures you did, the meanings they have for you, and your feelings about them. I want the rest of the family to share any questions when each person is finished.

IV. Concluding Statement

I think this exercise has helped us understand your family as it is now by remembering your past together. Linda, you became aware that you and Keith were never in a picture together, even before Ruth was born. I'm wondering whether you'd like to take some time now to tell us how you're feeling about that realization.

V. Worksheet

Childhood memory

TECHNIQUE

Positive Connotations

I. Source

Based on Selvini Palazzoli, M., Boscolo, L., Cecchin, G., & Prata, G. (1978). *Paradox and counterparadox: A new model in the therapy of the family in schizophrenic transaction.* New York: Jason Aronson.

II. Brief Description

Positive connotations involves the therapist's giving paradoxical prescriptions to a family regarding the members' behavior toward the presenting problem. The therapist relabels the symptom as a strength, and the family's dysfunctional responses to the symptom as healthy. The family is also advised to make no changes in how the members interact over the problem, since the problem is so useful to the family.

III. Initial Statement

I have to admire this family's closeness and drive to stay together. Anita, you, Kim, and Mark are working the hardest of all. Your constant fighting must be exhausting for you, but you're willing to keep it up so that you can have a close-knit family. And I can see that the rest of you appreciate their efforts. Your taking sides and arguing with each other about their fights keep everyone in the family involved. This family would fall apart if you ever stopped fighting.

IV. Concluding Statement

It's vital that you all continue to fight. The exhaustion and tension you experience is the price you pay for having such a close family. Remember, the family that fights together stays together.

V. Worksheet

Meta-rules

TECHNIQUE

Positive Double Bind

I. Source
Based on Luthman, S. G., & Kirschenbaum, M. (1974). *The dynamic family.* Palo Alto, CA: Science & Behavior Books.

II. Brief Description
A positive double bind is a message presented to a family by the therapist that is generated from the family's resistance. The therapist translates the energy back to the family in another way, which gives family members no alternative but to respond positively if they want to be consistent with their basic way of interacting.

III. Initial Statement
Keith, I'm sure all these reasons you offer for not continuing are valid, and perhaps you feel you aren't getting what you came for. However, if we look at the other side, every time we get close to feelings, which we did a moment ago with Linda and Anita, these feelings are avoided. Now, since you are a family committed to learning and growing, you will want to take this opportunity to explore this avoidance pattern and learn from it.

IV. Concluding Statement
I'm glad that you've made the decision to explore your avoidance behavior.

V. Worksheet
Journal format

TECHNIQUE

Positive Reinforcement

I. Source

Based on Brown, J., & Christensen, D. (1986). *Family therapy: Theory and practice.* Pacific Grove, CA: Brooks/Cole.

II. Brief Description

The key to this exercise is to catch your spouse or child doing something nice. It's a behavior-exchange procedure that involves partners' observing each other carefully, then clearly acknowledging, verbally or nonverbally, when they catch the other saying or doing something that gives them a good feeling.

III. Initial Statement

Keith and Linda, I'd like the two of you to try something that will help you be aware of each other and not take for granted each other's good points. With this technique, you give each other immediate positive reinforcement. It's quite simple. Observe each other, and whenever you catch the other person saying or doing something that gives you a good feeling, let them know. You can let the other person know simply by telling them or you can do something. Your response has to be immediate.

IV. Concluding Statement

I'd like you to begin trying positive reinforcement in our session today. So, if your spouse does something that sparks a good feeling for you, acknowledge it immediately. Next week we can discuss how this change has affected your relationship.

V. Guideline

Discipline

TECHNIQUE

Prescribing the Symptom

I. Source
Based on Rabkin, R. (1977). *Strategic psychotherapy.* New York: Basic Books.

II. Brief Description
With this technique, the therapist encourages the client's maladaptive behavior or symptom. This technique puts the client in the unpleasant position of maintaining a negative behavior, therefore demonstrating that the behavior can be voluntarily controlled.

III. Initial Statement
Keith, for the next week please continue dropping your socks and underwear on the floor, but in addition leave all your dirty clothes in a pile on the bedroom floor. Linda, I know you take great pride in your housekeeping, but do not pick up anything at all. Just leave it there—don't even put it in the laundry basket. Linda, I expect you will become more and more annoyed as the week goes by. And Keith, you can expect Linda to be angry with you and on your case most of the week.

IV. Concluding Statement
Do faithfully what I'm asking of you this week, and next week we'll discuss how my instructions affected your relationship.

V. Worksheet
Expectations

TECHNIQUE

Pretend

I. Source

Based on Madanes, C. (1982). *Strategic family therapy.* San Francisco: Jossey-Bass.

II. Brief Description

Pretend techniques are paradoxical interventions that use play, fantasy, and humor to help the family overcome resistance and work through a problem. Using make-believe as a mode of communication is especially appropriate for children, because they can understand and enjoy it. These interventions are flexible, enjoyable, and effective.

III. Initial Statement

Ruth, I realize that it must be very painful every time your head starts hurting at bedtime. Your parents have said that you start moaning, and you keep getting louder and louder until your mom comes in. Usually by that time, your mom is angry. What I'd like to do right now is to play a little game. Even though you don't have a headache, just pretend to have one. I want you to moan and get louder and louder, just the way you always do at bedtime. Then, Mom, you can come in and act as if Ruth has a headache. And Ruth, you get to pretend to have your headache again. Mom is going to come in and give you a hug and a kiss for doing such a good job, and you're going to give her a hug and a kiss back.

IV. Concluding Statement

Keith and Linda, sometimes when we pretend that a symptom is real, it is hard for the person to go back to real life and still continue to act as though the symptoms were real. So the symptom disappears. If it's only a pretend symptom, then it can't be a real one. In addition to getting rid of the headaches, this pretending has accomplished a lot more. Your daughter's behavior has improved, and both of you are interacting in a more effective way as parents.

V. Materials

Family set of puppets: mother, father, sons, daughters

TECHNIQUE

Psychodrama

I. Source
Based on Blatner, A., & Blatner, A. (1988). *Foundations of psychodrama: History, theory, and practice.* New York: Springer.

II. Brief Description
Psychodrama is an enactment technique that involves a family's working issues out for themselves by using their own creative process to set the scene and enact a conflict, confrontation, or encounter. The scene can be replayed from the past or something that the family contemplates doing in the future.

III. Initial Statement
We're going to look at the problem this morning in a different way. Anita, I'd like you to reenact the scene this morning between you and Linda. Anita, please set the stage. Move the chairs and tables around to represent the room the conflict took place in. Tell us what the room looks like. Describe Linda as you see her. The next step is to choose one of us to play Linda. I'll direct you in your drama. You'll start out playing yourself, Anita, and I may switch you to play Linda. You'll also be given a chance to talk about what happened, after which the rest of the family will be given a chance to share.

IV. Concluding Statement
I want Anita to hear from the rest of the family what feelings the drama evoked in you. Try not to give advice or offer opinions to either Anita or Linda. Just tell us what the scene meant to you.

V. Guideline
Psychodrama

TECHNIQUE

Quid pro Quo

I. *Source*

Based on Jackson, D. D. (1977). Family Rules: Marital Quid Pro Quo. In P. Watzlawick & J. H. Weakland (Eds.), *The interracial view: Studies at the Mental Research Institute, Palo Alto, 1965–1974.* New York: Norton.

II. *Brief Description*

This technique can help improve a stressful relationship between two people in a family. The clients are to fill out cards specifying what behavior they want from one another (see the quid pro quo worksheet in Part Three). They then exchange cards and negotiate until they establish an agreement.

III. *Initial Statement*

Linda and Keith, I would like each of you to fill out these cards and then exchange them with each other. Next to *what*, you should each write a description of what you want the other person to do. Then, after *when*, write down the place and the conditions in which the action should take place. Next, you each need to sign your initials and exchange the cards. I would like you to read them aloud. We will then decide *how long* these behaviors should occur. If you each agree to honor the request, initial it. Otherwise, we will bargain in order to reach agreement.

IV. *Concluding Statement*

Now that you have both agreed to meet each other's requests, your homework will be to follow through on them. I would like you to post these requests in a place where you will see them often. We will follow up on the results next session.

V. *Worksheet*

Quid pro quo cards

TECHNIQUE

Reframing

I. Source
Based on Hanna, S., & Brown, J. (1995). *The practice of family therapy: Key elements across models.* Pacific Grove, CA: Brooks/Cole.

II. Brief Description
Reframing is the act of relabeling an event or situation so as to provide a more constructive view of it. Reframing can change family perspectives and, ultimately, family behavior. The technique of reframing is often used to shed a more positive light on what was originally thought of as a bad situation. Frequently, a change in perception leads to a change in behavior.

III. Initial Statement
I am going to offer you a different view of Mark's disruptive behavior. I think Mark is acting out in school in order to protect you, his mom and dad. Mark has figured out that the two of you need protection from the problems that exist between you. Mark's problems at school bring the two of you together as you struggle to deal with him.

IV. Concluding Statement
Consider this a possible explanation for what is happening in your family. When families begin to look at situations in a new, positive light, change is frequently a result.

V. Worksheet
Relabeling

TECHNIQUE

Rejunction

I. Source
Based on Boszormenyi-Nagy, I., & Framo, S. (Eds.). (1965). *Intensive family therapy*. New York: Harper & Row.

II. Brief Description
Rejunction entails an effort by one family member to reconcile a relationship with another family member. The process involves taking the risk of breaking through barriers of mistrust between family members and openly communicating with each other. Rejunction also involves moving past old family scripts.

III. Initial Statement
Linda, I would like to hear you tell Anita that you really want to try to work things out between the two of you. You told Keith in front of all of us that you want to make a fresh start and try to get along with Anita. Now, I would like you to tell Anita exactly what you would like to do to bring the two of you closer together.

IV. Concluding Statement
Linda, I asked you to take a risk and explain to Anita how you are going to try to work out your differences. Sometimes, one person has to take the plunge and try to make up with another person. Doing so takes a lot of courage, but it is important to build trust between two people who have been at odds with each other.

V. Worksheet
Forgiveness

TECHNIQUE

Restructuring

I. Source
Based on Umbarger, C. C. (1983). *Structural family therapy.* New York: Grune & Stratton.

II. Brief Description
Restructuring is altering the usual functioning of the family structure. Restructuring may involve changing family members' roles, so that what was cozy and comfortable before becomes new and challenging. The purpose is to recognize dysfunction and come up with healthier ways of reacting to one another.

III. Initial Statement
Keith and Linda, sometimes family members become so used to relating to one another in a certain way that they stick with this comfortable routine even though they realize there's a problem, and their usual ways are no longer working. Usually, having a routine way of relating to one another provides security in the family by defining roles and setting limits. However, occasionally the routine becomes too rigid and actually harms family relationships. We want to change the family roles and some rules, so members who are not used to communicating with one another, like Linda and Anita, are forced to communicate. Our goal is to get every member to relate to one another.

IV. Concluding Statement
The goal of this exercise is to help you find new, healthier ways of communicating. I think it is obvious to all of us here that Keith's constant babying and giving in to Anita are hurting the family. Your way of relating to each other, Keith and Anita, also forms an alliance between the two of you against Linda and leaves her out in the cold. Restructuring has forced Linda and Anita to deal directly with each other without involving Keith.

V. Worksheet
Family reconstruction

TECHNIQUE

Reverse Role-Play

I. Source
Based on Barker, R. (1984). *Treating couples in crisis.* New York: Free Press.

II. Brief Description
Reverse role playing helps families to refocus by allowing them to see others' opinions from a different vantage point. Each person is asked to assume the role of his or her spouse. Then that person discusses a single problem in the relationship from the other person's viewpoint. People are often surprised at how accurately their spouses can present the other viewpoint. People are also surprised at how their own logic and grievances sound coming out of their spouses' mouths.

III. Initial Statement
Now, Linda and Keith, tomorrow night at 8:00 you've agreed to try the role reversal exercise. Linda, you imagine you are Keith. Discuss one problem about your relationship, pretending you are him. Become just like him and give his side of the argument. Try to win the argument for him. Keith, you do the same. Pretend you are Linda and act just as she does in a discussion. Give her point of view just as she would. I suggest you limit the exercise to ten minutes. Then take a few minutes to be apart. After a short wait, get together and talk over how it sounded to hear yourself from the other's viewpoint. Let's try it here!

IV. Concluding Statement
You both sounded pretty convincing to me. Linda, do you think Keith portrayed you accurately? How about you, Keith—what did you think of Linda's portrayal of you? Sometimes you get a new perspective by hearing your own words come out of your spouse's mouth.

V. Guideline
Reverse role playing

TECHNIQUE

Role Playing

I. Source

Based on Thompson, C. L., & Rudolph, L. B. (1991). *Counseling children* (3rd ed.). Pacific Grove, CA: Brooks/Cole.

II. Brief Description

Role playing can be used with adults and children in order to define a problem. The therapist asks the members to re-create a situation. Children often have trouble describing exactly what occurred in a particular situation, especially one involving interpersonal problems with parents, teachers, or peers. Role playing can provide children and adults insight into others' perceptions of their behavior.

III. Initial Statement

I noticed Mark is having difficulty explaining why he and his mother argue constantly. I would like Mark to act out a situation with me, and I'll act like his mother. Mark, I want you to show me exactly how you ask your mother, for instance, to take you to get ice cream. Talk to me exactly as you would if you were talking to her.

IV. Concluding Statement

When Mark and I were role-playing, it became obvious that Mark's manner of demanding things puts both of you on edge and leads to further conflicts. This week I want Mark to practice asking for things the way we rehearsed a few minutes ago. Next session, we'll talk about how it went.

V. Guideline

Role playing

TECHNIQUE

Ropes

I. Source
Based on Satir, V., & Baldwin, M. (1983). *Satir step by step: A guide to creating change in families*. Palo Alto, CA: Science & Behavior Books.

II. Brief Description
The therapist uses ropes to connect people in the room according to their relationships. The ropes show distance, tension, and entanglements among members. This technique involves helping the family to begin reorganizing and reducing these problems.

III. Initial Statement
Keith and Linda, I've watched your family, and I want you to try something. I'm going to connect each of you to every other family member with ropes tied around your wrists. This exercise will let us physically see where the tension and entanglements are. As you experience resistance in real life, express it with tension on your rope between you and that person.

IV. Concluding Statement
This exercise was intended to demonstrate physically the tension and entanglements within family. As you can see, Anita's rope was extremely tight with Linda and also entangled with her dad's. This tension uses a great deal of energy.

V. Materials
Ten 15-foot pieces of rope
One 50-foot piece of rope

TECHNIQUE

Rules Identification

I. *Source*
Based on Satir, V. (1972). *Peoplemaking*. Palo Alto, CA: Science & Behavior Books.

II. *Brief Description*
Rules are an extremely influential force in family life, and an understanding of them can be very enlightening. Unspoken rules may be at the source of many family problems. Rules of which some family members are unaware, as well as rules that have become irrelevant as the family develops, need to be clarified and discussed.

III. *Initial Statement*
With the whole family here, let's find out about your family's rules. First, elect a secretary; that person will write all the rules down. Don't get into any arguments about whether they're right or whether they're being obeyed. No one should try to catch anybody. Everyone gets a say. Now that you've written down all your family's rules, let's look at them more carefully. Are all the rules clear, or are some difficult for some of you to understand? Do any of the rules seem unfair? Why don't you go ahead now and ask the rulemakers to explain those rules to you. Now look to see which rules are still up to date. Are your rules helping the family, or are they making it difficult to get things done? One more question: What process can you work out for discussing and making changes in the rules?

IV. *Concluding Statement*
You've put together your family's set of rules. You've cleaned up some misunderstood rules and thrown out some old ones. You may not all agree with the rules all the time, but you have all figured out exactly what they are.

V. *Worksheet*
Meta-rules

TECHNIQUE

Rules of Interaction

I. *Source*
Based on Satir, V. (1967). *Conjoint family therapy.* Palo Alto, CA: Science & Behavior Books.

II. *Brief Description*
To decrease the likelihood of chaos in the therapy session, the therapist sets up rules of interaction. These rules include the following, among others: One person and only one speaks at a time. No one may speak for another person. Everyone speaks so that everyone else can hear what is being said. Each therapist must come up with his or her own set of rules of interaction.

III. *Initial Statement*
Before we begin this session, I want to set up some rules for us to follow. First, I want you to speak so that everyone can hear what you are saying. Second, no one is to interrupt when someone is speaking. You will have a turn to express yourself and your concerns. Third, I want to hear what each of you has to say; therefore, no one will speak for another person. Finally, it is absolutely necessary that you all be here for each session in order to interact with one another.

IV. *Concluding Statement*
Before our session comes to an end, I would like to share with you what I have observed. Today I think we all have seen that part of the family's problem is communication. Keith, you seem to talk for your son. Anita, you speak so softly that it's difficult for anyone to hear you. Check what happens at home this week, and tell me about it next session.

V. *Worksheets*
Meta-rules
Rules

TECHNIQUE

Sculpting

I. Source
Based on McGoldrick, M., Pearce, J. K., & Giordano, J. (1982). *Ethnicity and family therapy.* New York: Guilford Press.

II. Brief Description
The technique of sculpting was developed for use with families where members are in conflict. The goal is to allow the whole family to see how one of its members physically positions the family. A sculptor from the family places each member according to his or her perceptions. Each member of the family can act as the sculptor if time permits.

III. Initial Statement
I would like all of you in the family to try something that will help you to see your differences more clearly. It involves one of you sculpting the members of your family as you see them. The family will not be speaking, so it will be like a photograph. After that, I would like you to change the picture to the way you want it to look. Be creative in your changes. As the family members are positioned by the sculptor, their reactions to the changes are encouraged. After the family sculpture is completed, I will ask each of you to go into each other's original sculpture and make the changes you believe to be better.

IV. Concluding Statement
Because this technique of sculpting is very powerful, I want you to spend time discussing and sharing your experiences.

V. Guideline
Psychodrama

TECHNIQUE

Self-Disclosure

I. Source
Based on Selekman, M. (1993). *Pathways to change.* New York: Guilford Press.

II. Brief Description
Self-disclosure consists of talking about yourself, your feelings, and your thoughts in relation to some event or situation. Most of the time we describe events as if we were not even involved.

III. Initial Statement
Keith and Linda, I have noticed that each of you has some difficulty in talking about yourself. I hope we can identify some important issues and personal burdens that you can share. Some rules should be followed when self-disclosing. You can talk about yourself, how you view yourself, how you relate to interpersonal problems, how another's actions are affecting you, and how you react to another's actions. Keith, tell us how you are feeling right now. It's easier to start with "I feel . . . ."

IV. Concluding Statement
I would like each of you to try this with someone in your family this coming week.

V. Worksheet
Johari window

TECHNIQUE

Siding

I. Source
Based on Ferber, A., Mendelsohn, M., & Napier, A. (1972). *The book of family therapy.* New York: Jason Aronson.

II. Brief Description
The therapist's goal in using this technique is to maintain a sense of impartiality among the group as a whole while bonding with each family member. The therapist asks each family member to express a view to the family. The therapist then expands on that viewpoint so that the other members sense the therapist's support for that family member—and the rest of the family as well.

III. Initial Statement
Each of you has a special place in this family. I would like each of you to tell us exactly why you feel you are valuable to your family. In other words, tell us what you do to help everyone out and why. Linda, let's begin with you.

IV. Concluding Statement
You have all had a chance to share with the group the ways you believe you help the family. I wanted each of you to get a clear picture of how the other people in the group try to do things for the good of the family. Even Ruth does a good job at making you all laugh when she tries to imitate Mark. The purpose of this activity was to help you all understand and appreciate one another a little more.

V. Worksheet
Dimensions of support

TECHNIQUE

Skeleton Keys

I. Source
Based on de Shazer, S. (1985). *Keys to the solution in brief therapy.* New York: Norton.

II. Brief Description
Skeleton keys are formulas that describe structured interventions used to stimulate healthy patterns of behavior. Examples include "write/read/burn," "structured fight," "do something different," and "overcoming the urge." These structured interventions are primarily designed to distract a person from old, unhealthy behavioral patterns by prescribing new specific steps for the person to follow.

III. Initial Statement
Keith and Linda, sometimes when a couple fights, each partner is so focused on telling his or her side that little listening or understanding takes place. So what we are going to do is to provide some structure to your fighting. When an argument is about to begin, flip a coin to see who goes first. That person talks for ten minutes, uninterrupted. Then it is the other's turn for ten minutes. After that, ten minutes of silence occurs before another round begins.

IV. Concluding Statement
By being forced to observe what is going on in certain situations or by having certain behaviors brought to your attention, you are given a key to unlock the solution. Once you achieve understanding, you can work on a solution that is agreeable to both of you.

V. Guideline
Skeleton keys

TECHNIQUE

Sociogram

I. *Source*
Based on Leveton, E. (1977). *Psychodrama for the timid clinician.* New York: Springer.

II. *Brief Description*
The psychodramatic sociogram is a physical representation or picture of a person's relationships in life. Used to explore one's relationships, this living picture represents a person's place and position in relation to family, friends, school- or workmates, or society.

III. *Initial Statement*
Keith, Jr., I'd like to explore where you feel you fit in your family. You can sit or stand in the center of the room. I'll stay with you. From there I want you to put people, family members or friends past or present, around you. Place these people around you according to how close to or far away you feel they are to you. If you feel close to someone who maybe doesn't return that feeling, you could place that person close but have his or her back turned toward you. Take your time and think about how you feel. When they're all in place I want you to give words to your picture. Speak one sentence for each person in the way he or she would speak to you.

IV. *Concluding Statement*
Now that you've finished, Keith Jr., I'd like to share your feelings about the picture you made.

V. *Guideline*
Psychodrama

TECHNIQUE

Speaker's Chair

I. *Source*
Based on Haley, J. (1987). *Problem-solving therapy* (2nd ed.). San Francisco: Jossey-Bass.

II. *Brief Description*
This technique may be useful for a family in which everyone constantly interrupts one another. A specific speaker's chair is designated, and only the person sitting in that chair may speak. The therapist might also designate a speaker's object, like the ancient talking stick or a rubber ball.

III. *Initial Statement*
Keith, after listening to what has been going on for the last ten minutes, I have noticed that you never allow other family members to finish what they are saying before you interrupt them. I'm going to get an extra chair, put it right here, and call it the speaker's chair. Only the person sitting in the speaker's chair may speak. Everyone else must listen without any kind of interruption. I promise that everyone will have the chance to sit in the chair.

IV. *Concluding Statement*
Since everyone has had the chance to sit in the speaker's chair, I would like to hear from each one of you what it was like to talk without being interrupted. From what everyone has told me, you all liked sitting in the speaker's chair.

V. *Worksheet*
Conflict resolution

TECHNIQUE

Storytelling

I. *Source*
Based on Gardner, J. (1971). *Therapeutic communication with children: Mutual storytelling.* New York: Science House.

II. *Brief Description*
Storytelling is a useful way of temporarily surrendering the expert position. The therapist can make a point indirectly, using a personal experience, while modeling self-disclosure. The therapist's sharing personal experiences encourages involvement.

III. *Initial Statement*
All this talk of trying to bring up your children to be good, responsible people has me thinking about how it was when I was a kid. It must have been hard for my parents. One day, my kindergarten teacher said we could take home baby gerbils—if we brought in a note from a parent. I went home and asked to have a pet gerbil, but my parents right away said no without elaborating, though I persisted in asking for an explanation. Since I never was given a reason, I wrote my own permission note and folded it up so that only a blank square was visible. Then I asked my dad to write his name there so I could practice penmanship. The next day I brought the note to school, and although the teacher gave me a gerbil, my parents made me take it right back to school. Do you know, to this day, I don't know why they didn't want me to have a gerbil.

IV. *Concluding Statement*
Sometimes parents assume that children won't take no for an answer because they are being stubborn or just plain selfish. I think that children are naturally curious, and they understand a lot more than we give them credit for. Perhaps part of the reason Mark disobeys you is that he doesn't understand the purpose of your setting limits with him. Do you think that Mark might listen if you took some time to help him understand the reasons you set limits?

V. *Guideline*
Self-disclosure

TECHNIQUE

Straightforward Directives

I. Source
Based on Haley, J. (1987). *Problem solving therapy for effective family therapy* (2nd ed.). San Francisco: Jossey-Bass.

II. Brief Description
A straightforward directive is an order or request the therapist makes to a family member. For example, if the therapist wants a child to stop interrupting the parent, the therapist tells the child, "Stop!" The instructions of a straightforward directive need to be very clear—for example, "I want the family to do the following: You are to . . . ." After giving a straightforward directive, at the next session the therapist should always ask family members whether they did the task.

III. Initial Statement
Linda and Anita, I would like to give you an assignment to carry out over the next week to help you understand each other better. Anita, every evening after dinner I'd like you to spend fifteen minutes telling Linda what your day was like. Linda, during those fifteen minutes, I want you to give Anita your undivided attention. I also want you to compliment and encourage Anita about what she's done well that day.

IV. Concluding Statement
Linda and Anita, we've agreed today that you will spend at least fifteen minutes together each evening, trying to communicate in a civil and caring manner.

V. Guideline
Encouragement

TECHNIQUE

Systemic Hypothesis

I. Source
Based on Anderson & Bayarozzi (1983). The use of family myths as an end to strategic therapy. *Journal of Family Therapy (5)*, 145–154.

II. Brief Description
The therapist develops a systemic hypothesis based on the perceived cognitive map held by the family, and it will include what usually causes the family to stumble. The therapist can test the logic of this map through circular questioning. If the hypothesis is not accurate, another is chosen, and the order of questions is then changed to test the new hypothesis.

III. Initial Statement
A family that becomes stuck around an issue is often clinging to a faulty belief, or a map that isn't needed anymore. Let's test your belief that Keith Sr. and Anita must eat your stewed tomatoes. If we find out what meaning this has to both you and Keith, you can better understand its significance and move beyond it.

IV. Concluding Statement
We have examined the source of your beliefs about eating stewed tomatoes to get a better sense of their logic and to see whether other choices can be applied. You are now ready to use the new map you've chosen to get unstuck and move beyond this issue.

V. Guideline
Circular questions

TECHNIQUE

Taking Sides

I. *Source*
Based on Zuk, G. H. (1981). *Family therapy: A triadic based approach* (rev. ed.). New York: Human Sciences Press.

II. *Brief Description*
When taking sides, the therapist identifies an area where the family is stuck and brings up the issue for discussion in the session. The therapist fans the fire by taking sides—first with one family member, then another—quickly disengaging before the family can draw the therapist into any coalition. However, while the therapist is engaged, he or she assumes leadership, takes control, issues directives, mediates, and sets limits.

III. *Initial Statement*
Linda, I think you want Keith to take over and tell all the children what to do all the time. Keith, you believe that Linda is supposed to control the children and that it's all her fault when the kids misbehave. Kids, you are all just playing one parent against the other—trying to get your way and make your parents mad at each other.

IV. *Concluding Statement*
Each of you needs to make some decisions about how you are going to live together for the next several years. I can't decide how you're going to behave, and I can't take sides on issues within the family.

V. *Worksheet*
Meta-rules

TECHNIQUE

Telegram

I. *Source*

Based on Stevens, J. O. (1981). *Awareness: Exploring, experimenting, experiencing.* New York: Bantam.

II. *Brief Description*

For five minutes, members in a family are to send messages to each other in two- or three-word sentences—the way they would if writing a telegram. Family members are asked to be aware of how they feel when they receive a message containing only the most vital and significant information another member wants them to hear. The sender also clarifies for him- or herself the message he or she wants to send.

III. *Initial Statement*

For the next five minutes, whatever each of you in the family says to one another must be expressed in two or three words, as if you were sending a telegram. Think about the most important thoughts and feelings you want to convey, and put them into only the most important and significant words. For example, you might say, "Mom, love," or "Dad, talk to Mom." This exercise will help you clarify your thoughts and feelings and will make it easier for you to phrase them. You will be able to stop worrying about saying something in just the right words and speak your thoughts more clearly.

IV. *Concluding Statement*

By condensing your thoughts and feelings into a minimum number of words, you were able to convey your messages much more clearly. You can now use this as a first step when you want to communicate a message.

V. *Worksheet*

Telegrams

TECHNIQUE

Tickling of Defenses

I. Source
Based on Ackerman, N. (1958). *The psychodynamics of family life: Diagnosis and treatment of family relationships.* New York: Basic Books.

II. Brief Description
Tickling of defenses involves exposing incongruent verbal and nonverbal expressions. Family members are prompted to explore deeper levels of communication, while the therapist observes behaviors as well as listens to the family interactions. The therapist challenges members whose words are not congruent with their actions.

III. Initial Statement
Keith, you just told Linda that you hate it when she says that you don't take an active role in raising the children and that it really makes you angry when she accuses you of not caring about them. Yet, you were smiling when you made the statement and even chuckled when you used the word *hate*. *Hate* is a very strong word, and the emotion that usually goes with it is anger. I'm wondering whether you were aware of this discrepancy. And Linda, I'd like to see whether you can recall any times when you might have noticed Keith smiling when he is angry.

IV. Concluding Statement
Keith, my purpose in pointing out this discrepancy was not to put you on the spot, but to make you aware that your actions were not agreeing with the emotions that you were expressing. Often, when people have difficulty dealing with or expressing an emotion, they cover it up. I was concerned that your laughing took away from how strongly you really felt.

V. Worksheet
Nonverbal cues

TECHNIQUE

Time Out

I. Source

Based on Piercy, F., Sprenkle, D., et al. (1986). *Family therapy source book.* New York: Guilford Press.

II. Brief Description

Time out is a method used to decrease the occurrence of negative behavior. An individual might be asked to go get a soda or to get something for the therapist, so that negative behavior does not continue to be reinforced. The therapist can provide these general guidelines for the use of time out at home:

1. The child should be sent to a room other than his or her bedroom.
2. The child should be given a definite amount of time to be in the time-out area without any activity (five minutes for young children, fifteen minutes for older children).
3. No scolding or punishing can be done on the way to the time-out room.
4. The parent must not spank the child during the time out.

III. Initial Statement

We talked about reinforcement today. Linda, you say that you are frustrated by Mark's behavior, and you feel guilty after you yell at him. This week, when Mark acts up, I would like you to give him a time out. That means that you simply put him in another room, the bathroom or the dining room, for fifteen minutes. Be sure that Mark knows that for the whole fifteen minutes he may not misbehave, or you start the time again from zero.

IV. Concluding Statement

I would like you to use these methods consistently throughout the week. Next week, Linda, please give me a full account of how this worked. Tell me whether time out was a more successful disciplinary measure than yelling at Mark.

V. Guideline

Time out

TECHNIQUE

Touch

I. *Source*
Based on Satir, V., & Baldwin, M. (1983). *Satir step by step: A guide to creating change in families*. Palo Alto, CA: Science & Behavior Books.

II. *Brief Description*
The word *touch* in family therapy refers to physical contact that respects the client's individual boundaries. A pat on the back or a handshake is an example of touch that can be used to show support for the person being contacted or act as a sign of support to another family member observing the contact. Touch allows respectful intimacy to take place.

III. *Initial Statement*
Keith and Linda, in the next few minutes we have spent together I can hear the frustration and isolation everyone is feeling. What I would like you to do now is have the family move closer together in our circle and hold hands. Hold hands and just be with one another. Know that although your frustrations are very real to you, you are not alone. We are all here together. As we close our session tonight I want you to take part in a group hug.

IV. *Concluding Statement*
Between now and the next session, hug or shake the hand of someone in the family at least twice a day, and then write down how you felt or what you thought. Very real communication can go on without any words.

V. *Worksheet*
Dimensions of support

TECHNIQUE

Transactional Patterns

I. Source

Based on Minuchin, S., & Fishman, H. C. (1981). *Family therapy techniques.* Cambridge, MA: Harvard University Press.

II. Brief Description

This technique attempts to change a family's transactional patterns in order to change the dysfunctional family structure. The therapist brings to light the covert rules governing a family's transactional patterns and then tries to alter the family's structure by physically altering the distance and proximity among family members.

III. Initial Statement

As I listen to all of you talk, I'm getting the idea that you have a lot of rules in your family that you are not aware of. For instance, Linda, you're sitting way over there, far away from your husband. Keith, I'd like you to come over here and sit next to your wife. Keith Jr., since you and Mark are such good buddies, I'm going to put your little sister, Ruth, between you. Now the two of you can include her in your conversation. Linda and Keith, the two of you can get to know each other again, as a couple, since Ruth is off with the boys for a while.

IV. Concluding Statement

I wonder if you saw what was happening before. Keith and Linda, you were trying to protect Ruth from her big brother, but in doing so, you were letting her come between you as a couple. Meanwhile Keith Jr. and Mark were sticking together so much because they were feeling left out of your threesome. But these were things that no one in the family was able to talk about. You can have your time without always including one of the children.

V. Worksheet

Family reconstruction

TECHNIQUE

Triadic Exercises

I. Source
Based on Satir, V., & Baldwin, M. (1983). *Satir step by step: A guide to creating change in families.* Palo Alto, CA: Science & Behavior Books.

II. Brief Description
Exercises that help us become aware of feelings and behaviors are important in fostering clear communication. In triadic exercises, two people engage in an interaction. A third observes and then offers feedback on the interaction to the two people.

III. Initial Statement
Keith, Linda, and Anita, we are going to concentrate for a while on becoming more aware of feelings in others and in ourselves. Two of you will talk for five minutes, while the third person observes. At the end of the time, the observer will say what feelings were communicated and how he or she felt not being a part of the conversation. The other two will also be asked to share their experiences.

IV. Concluding Statement
This exercise actually emphasizes two things. First, becoming more aware of feelings is vitally important for all of us. By being told how we convey our messages, we can make changes if necessary. Second, interactions in families are not always just between two people. Sometimes three or more people are concerned in a conversation.

V. Guideline
Self-disclosure

TECHNIQUE

Triangles

I. Source

Based on Satir, V. (1972). *Peoplemaking*. Palo Alto, CA: Science & Behavior Books.

II. Brief Description

With this technique, the client draws a circle for each family member, labeling each circle with a face (if the client is a small child) or a name. Each client or family member is to connect three family members by drawing three straight lines. The drawing will look like a triangle when finished. Usually, there is an "odd man out" in any triangle. This person can choose to do one of three things: break up the relationship between the other two by being an interested observer.

III. Initial Statement

Linda and Keith, you can learn more about your family and the way you treat each other by looking closely at the family in sets of three. On this piece of paper, I want each of you to draw three circles—one to represent you and two to represent the other family members. Label the circles so that you remember who everyone is. One person in a triangle is always the "odd man out." Anita, who are you in the triangle, odd man out or part of the remaining pair? Kim, how does it feel? Are you always odd man out or does your position change from time to time? Linda, what do you do when you are odd man out to try to be part of the pair?

IV. Concluding Statement

Triangles are very important to a family's operation, so we should understand how to make them work. In a triangle, equal attention cannot be paid to all members at the same time. Watch for this during the next week, and we can talk about it next session.

V. Materials

Pad of blank paper
Ten pencils

TECHNIQUE

Typical Day

I. Source
Based on Grunwald, B. B., & McAbee, H. M. (1985). *Guiding the family: Practical counseling techniques.* Muncie, IN: Accelerated Development.

II. Brief Description
All behavior is purposeful. The way a family behaves and interacts provides the therapist with important information about family members' goals and motivations. Each day is unique and yet has many similarities. Each family member needs to record the day's activity and then bring it to the next session.

III. Initial Statement
As I listen to all of you in the family describe how you interact with one another, I can see that a greater understanding of what's happening would be helpful. Each of you is a unique person, and you do very different things during your day. I want you to begin to observe your behavior by keeping a detailed, written account of a typical day. Record all events from the time you get up until you go to bed.

IV. Concluding Statement
I think observing behavior is more reliable than listening to words. By gathering information on your actions and reactions to the events of a typical day, I can better help you sort out your life together. This will be helpful in resolving current conflicts as well as finding instructive ways of living with each other.

V. Worksheet
Typical day journal

TECHNIQUE

Unbalancing

I. Source

Based on Minuchin, S., & Fishman, H. D. (1981). *Family therapy techniques.* Cambridge, MA: Harvard University Press.

II. Brief Description

Unbalancing is aimed at shifting and changing the hierarchical relationships within a system or subsystem. In a therapeutic system, the therapist joins as the expert, immediately having an impact on the family's power structure. This power is not used until the therapist challenges and changes the family's structure by affiliating with one individual or subsystem at the expense of the others.

III. Initial Statement

Linda, it seems as though you think people should behave in a certain way, and Keith sees things differently. You know, Keith, Linda doesn't like the way you see people and life. She's also saying that you don't have feelings. It seems to me that you have feelings—anger, pain, grief, happiness. You just express your feelings differently from Linda. She is insisting that you are to act and be just like her. But why? Because you don't react like Linda doesn't make your behavior wrong—just different.

IV. Concluding Statement

Keith, even though you were hesitant to listen to me at first, by my being on your side against your wife, you've had a chance to experiment, and you have changed. Linda, I realize you were accustomed to seeing Keith as the problem, the one who couldn't express emotions and handle situations like you. I know you were confused when I took Keith's side against you, but I hope you realize that he is able to meet the challenge.

V. Worksheet

Journal format

TECHNIQUE

Use of Self

I. Source
Based on Whitaker, C. A., & Bumberry, W. M. (1988). *Dancing with the family: A symbolic-experimental approach.* New York: Brunner/Mazel.

II. Brief Description
A therapist understands others through his or her own experiences and past history. The main tool a therapist has to use with clients is the self. A therapist can provide insight to the family by sharing perceptions about the family's situation. This sharing is called the use of self.

III. Initial Statement
Linda, as I am listening to you tell your story about the conflicts you are having with Anita, I can't help but wonder if you have been through all this before during your own childhood. I know that my own childhood has had a strong influence on my relationships today. I often find myself experiencing the same conflicts over again, as I am sensitive to what has bothered me in the past. When faced with similar conflicts now, I find myself reacting in the same way I did in the past, even though I know it did not work for me then. I wonder if that's what's happening with you.

IV. Concluding Statement
Our pasts often affect our current lives in a variety of ways. I believe sharing some of myself will help you benefit from my experiences.

V. Worksheet
Johari window

TECHNIQUE

Value Assessment

I. Source
Based on Sherman, R., & Fredman, N. (1986). *Handbook of structured techniques in marriage and family therapy.* New York: Brunner/Mazel.

II. Brief Description
The value assessment comparison exercise is based on the assumption that awareness and expression of value, which affect relationships among people, are important in understanding the psychosocial systems people form. This exercise can be used in marital or family therapy to provide insight into interpersonal perception, communication, and system balance.

III. Initial Statement
Keith and Linda, I'm going to give you an assignment for next week. I'd like the two of you to go home and write out a list of the things, objects, and activities that you consider most important to you. Then write out another list representing your spouse's values. You can make the lists as long or as short as you like, but don't show each other your lists or discuss them until we meet again next week. Then we'll compare the lists and discuss any differences of opinion.

IV. Concluding Statement
You may find some surprises next week when we review your lists.

V. Worksheet
Expectations

TECHNIQUE

Video Playback

I. Source
Based on Haley, J. (1971). *Changing families.* New York: Grune & Stratton.

II. Brief Description
Video playback is a way of capturing the content, affect, and context of a situation. It allows a family to see body language and gestures, thus gaining further understanding. Video makes it possible to stand back, experience the feelings, and observe what actually happened. For some clients, it's like looking in a mirror.

III. Initial Statement
Keith, time and again I hear from your family that there's a lack of respect for one another. This concerns me. We're experiencing a blockage that we need to get through. I'd like to video our session for the next four weeks. During the last fifteen minutes of each session, we'll view part of the session. This way we'll get a glimpse of what is going on when we all communicate.

IV. Concluding Statement
Videotaping captures the real moment. No matter what happens, the film records it, and we can play it back bit by bit. Let's take a look at what happened.

V. Worksheet
Nonverbal cues

TECHNIQUE

Vulnerability Contract

I. Source
Based on Duhl, B. S. (1976). *The vulnerability contract: A tool for turning alienation into connection with couples, families, and groups.* Mexico City: First International Family Encounter.

II. Brief Description
The vulnerability contract is a contract between spouses that lists each one's worst fears and how the partner can recognize those fears. The contract specifies signals that the person and the spouse can come to recognize and specific actions to take when either spouse becomes aware of the signals.

III. Initial Statement
Keith and Linda, I would like the two of you to do a homework assignment this week. Come up with a contract for each of you that lists your worst times. Then, you will specify signals you are aware of that occur as these bad times happen. The contract will then specify what actions you two should undertake when these signals occur.

IV. Concluding Statement
Often, we just don't recognize when we are going through tough times. Identifying the signals of our difficult times, and actions to take when we observe these signals, allows us to be more helpful to one another.

V. Worksheet
Vulnerability contract

TECHNIQUE

Worst Alternative

I. *Source*
Based on Haley, J. (1986). *Uncommon therapy: The psychiatric techniques of Milton H. Erickson, M.D.* New York: Norton.

II. *Brief Description*
Providing a worst alternative involves suggesting that the family do something that you think they will probably find more unappealing than the problem itself or that will make what you really think they should do look attractive to them.

III. *Initial Statement*
Keith and Linda, the two of you seem to have a great deal of difficulty settling arguments. You continue to bicker and make snide remarks to each other about an argument you had weeks ago. This week, I would like you to go through the entire week arguing about old arguments. You are to constantly argue about arguing. Otherwise, you are not to speak to each other at any time: no good mornings, no dinner talk. This means no notes and no speaking through your children, either.

IV. *Concluding Statement*
When you come back next week, we'll take a look at how pleasant your week was, since you didn't have to speak with each other.

V. *Worksheet*
Problem solving

PART THREE

RESOURCES

WORKSHEETS

GUIDELINE

Behavioral Rehearsal

Source
From Davis, K. M. (1993). *Working with children*. Unpublished manuscript.

These general rules give the counselor an overview of the process. See the guidelines for role-playing and reverse role-playing for information about those techniques.

1. Behavioral rehearsal is to practice the person's plan, and to try a new behavior.
2. The person and counselor have role-played a conflict, using the person's typical way of behaving.
3. The person and counselor have reverse role-played, so the person can identify how the other person feels in the conflict.
4. The person and counselor have developed a plan for a constructive new behavior.
5. The counselor may model the plan for the person by actually showing the person how to behave in the new, more constructive way.
6. The person tries out the constructive new behavior, several times if necessary.
7. The counselor assumes the other person's role as revealed in the original role playing.
8. The person and counselor process the experience by doing a reality check on what has transpired.

GUIDELINE

Circular Questions

Source

Reprinted from Fleuridas, C., Nelson, J. S., & Rosenthal, D. M. (1986). The evolution of circular questions: Training family therapists. *Journal of Marital and Family Therapy, vol. 12.* Copyright © 1986 American Association for Marriage and Family Therapy. Reprinted with permission.

MAJOR CATEGORIES

Problem definition questions	*Sequence of intervention questions*	*Comparison and classification questions*	*Interventive questions*
What is the family's main concern?	When your mother and brother are fighting, what does your father do?	Who is the closest to whom?	What is something fun you did with your family this week? *(ask each member)*
Who agrees with you that this is the problem?		Who is most convinced that something is wrong? *(rank order)*	
What was the problem in the family then?	What does Dad's behavior mean to you?	How are you raising your children differently from the way your parents raised you?	How did your parents discipline you in the past? Was it effective?
How is that different from what the problem is now?	What is your explanation for this?		What did your family do the last time this happened?
What purpose does that problem serve?	How is Mom's behavior different? Describe what she used to do.	Who would act the most upset if this were to happen?	How often do you go out together? Alone? As a couple?
	What would this mean to you/her/him/them?	What is your explanation for this?	What do you think would be the most effective way to resolve this problem?

GUIDELINE

Communication

Source

Based on DeVito, J. (1995). *The interpersonal communication book* (7th ed.). Copyright © 1995 Joseph A. DeVito. Adapted with permission of Harper-Collins Publishers, Inc.

A number of barriers to good communication distort the world in which a family functions.

1. *Polarization:* A tendency to emphasize the extremes of a situation forces the family to accept one position or the other and does not allow individuals to move toward a central position.

2. *Intentional orientation:* This term describes the tendency to label people, objects, and events rather than to recognize how they actually are. This attitude freezes people into one position that becomes hard to refute.

3. *Bypassing:* This occurs when two people use different words but mean the same thing, or use the same words that have two different meanings. In each instance they bypass the true meaning.

4. *Fact Inference/Confusion:* To attribute truth to inferential statements made by family members causes confusion. Assuming you know the facts is different from actually knowing them.

5. *Allness:* There is no way for family members to know everything about each other. It is judgmental to make statements that convey that one knows everything about why another family member behaves in a certain way.

6. *Static evaluation:* In the ever-changing world of the family there is a tendency to believe that once a verbal statement is made it is always going to be true. In fact, enormous changes occur in the life of a family.

7. *Indiscrimination:* Individuals tend to accept stereotypes of groups of people, to attribute basic characteristics to them, and then to say that every person in that group has those characteristics.

GUIDELINE

Discipline I

Source

Adapted from Wolfgang, C. H., & Glickman, C. D. (1986). *Solving discipline problems: Strategies for classroom teaching* (2nd ed.). Copyright © 1986 Allyn & Bacon. Adapted with permission.

This chart presents two different models of discipline. For each, basic assumptions of motivation, overt parent behaviors, and covert parent behaviors are given.

Behavior Modification Discipline Model	Reality Discipline Model
• Deal with outward undesirable behavior	• Children are capable of being responsible
• Help child change behavior by using motivational reinforcers	• Love and self-worth are two basic needs
• Consequences primarily determine behavior	• Behavior problems result from these needs not being met
• Causes of behavior exist in the environment	• Person must make a commitment to responsible behavior
• Parents impact the situation through imitation, shaping, and contingency contract	• Confronting transgressions
• Use explicit modeling, forward and backward chaining, saturation, time out, rewards for reinforcement, and commands	• Asking *what* questions • Pressing for a plan • Agreeing on natural consequences
• Use conditioners in the form of material and verbal rewards	
• Select behavior to be changed	• Observing the child and situation
• Collect data and record baseline	• Assessing parents' action and child's success
• Identify appropriate reinforcers	
• Apply reinforcers, evaluate, and change reinforcers as necessary	• Start fresh by changing family and home organization or activities

GUIDELINE

Discipline II

Source

Adapted from Wolfgang, C. H., & Glickman, C. D. (1986). *Solving discipline problems: Strategies for classroom teaching* (2nd ed.). Copyright © 1986 Allyn & Bacon. Adapted with permission.

This chart presents two different models of discipline. Each approach tests some of the basic assumptions of motivation, overt parent behaviors, and covert parent behaviors.

Social Discipline Model	*Value Discipline Model*
• Children are decision-making social beings	• Values, emotion, and IQ influence behavior
• Misbehavior results from faulty reasoning about how to gain attention	• Value experience can diminish certain behavior
• All behavior is directed toward social goals	• Children can rationally choose and act on values
• Reality is what the child perceives it to be	
• Confront and challenge the child's behavior in a moderate manner	• Modeling
• Ask questions such as "Could it be that you want . . . ?"	• Questions
	• Listening carefully and patiently
• Use continual encouragement to increase confidence	• Clarifying responses
	• Formal exercises
• Give complete nonverbal attention	• Establish mood of acceptance
• Allow the child to exert appropriate power	• Develop respect for child's values
	• Focus attention on child's real-life issues
• Redirect toward a positive response	
• Give easy tasks to complete to increase self-esteem	

GUIDELINE

Empty Chair

Source

Based on Young, M. E. (1992). *Counseling methods and techniques: An eclectic approach.* New York: Merrill.

- The empty chair is a way of having a person talk to the self or someone else, rather than about oneself or another.

- Through enactments, the therapist helps the person express present feelings such as anger, sadness, love, and regret to real individuals who are imagined to be sitting in the empty chair.

- This technique can result in catharsis and greater awareness for the person.

- The therapist's interventions are centered on asking *what* and *how* questions in the here and now.

Steps in Using the Empty Chair

- The therapist must first tell the person that the therapist would like to try an experiment, and get the person's permission to proceed.

- When the person starts talking about someone, the therapist tells the person to imagine that the other person is sitting in the empty chair, and tells the person to talk to that other person.

- The person is encouraged to express feelings toward people around whom he or she has energy.

- Therapists must not be judgmental during the enactments. They must allow the person to freely cathart.

- During the enactment, the therapist may move the person from one chair to the other only when the person asks a question, makes an accusation, or is speaking in polarities.

- Therapists may ask questions beginning with *what* and *how*, and tell the person to be aware of nonverbals such as crying, tightening fists, sitting on hands, or hitting something.

- The point is for the therapist not to be judgmental and critical during the session.

- Let the person determine the direction of the session and allow the person to end the session when he or she is ready.

- At the end of the session the therapist should have the person state resentments, appreciations, and regrets toward anyone the person spoke with during the session.

GUIDELINE

Encouragement

Source

Based on Crabb, L., & Allender, D. (1984). *Encouragement: The key to caring*. Grand Rapids, MI: Zondervan Publishing House.

Real Encouragement

- Encouragement depends on positive motivation by the encourager and the wisdom to discern the needs of the other person accurately.
- Real encouragement is inspired by and spoken from a heart of love and directed toward another's fear.
- Real encouragement means not being afraid of getting involved in other people's lives in ways that may feel risky and uncomfortable to the encourager. It means acting out of love and in spite of personal fear that the encouragement may result in stress, tension, and a disruption of the present relationship between the encourager and the encouraged. The encourager reaches out to another in spite of the fear of rejection, ridicule, and anger from the person being encouraged.

Why Real Encouragement Is Difficult to Give and Receive

- People have a tendency to relate to others from behind defensive layers.
- Defenses keep us safe from the risks involved in authentically encouraging others.
- People withdraw to safety behind layers of criticism, analysis, gossip, interest, and perhaps concern while attempting to encourage others, if real encouragement feels too risky.
- People are inhibited from expressing authentic encouragement because they fear intimacy. People also fear creating tension and losing the safety and comfort of a relationship as it exists.

GUIDELINE

Extinction

Source

Based on Granvold, D. K. (Ed.). (1994). *Cognitive and behavioral treatment.* Pacific Grove, CA: Brooks/Cole.

Definition

Extinction is a process by which one person withholds attention from another who is acting inappropriately. It is enacted by removing all reinforcement and attention from the individual who is displaying the maladaptive or undesirable behavior. Extinction is achieved by consistently ignoring the target behavior.

Example

A child continually interrupts his parents as they speak to a friend. The parents may attend to the child's demands or just verbally rebuke the child for interrupting. Either way, the child is getting the parent's attention. The child continues to believe that future interruptions will result in getting the parent's attention. The child's interrupting behaviors may be stopped through the process of extinction.

Home-Based

Home-based practitioners need to realize that extinction is a trying, slow procedure. The person whose behavior is being targeted may be slow to change. The practitioner must be prepared to ignore the individual each time the undesirable behavior is presented, since inconsistent attendance to the behavior will reinforce it. All important people in the individual's life must cooperate. Home-based practitioners should be aware that initially the maladaptive behavior will increase as an expression of resistance to changing the behavior. For that reason, extinction should not be used when the behavior is likely to be hazardous to the child or others.

Example

An adolescent makes repeated cynical and demeaning remarks toward her mother during dinner. The father initially responds by asking the daughter to stop. He then asks her why she talks to her mother that way. Finally, he becomes angry and begins arguing with the daughter. This results in both parents' sending her from the table. The daughter gets the attention she desires. To stop the daughter's inappropriate behavior, the parents can tell their daughter that her words are hurtful and not presented in a way appropriate for discussion, and then continue to eat dinner. If the daughter persists, she will be told to leave the table, and that she may return when she can speak in a less hostile fashion. The parents do not respond to her until she changes her behavior. An important point is that they do not demean or insult her.

GUIDELINE

Genogram

Source

Based on McGoldrick, M., & Gerson, R. (1985). *Genogram in family assessment*. New York: Norton.

A genogram is a format for drawing a family tree that records information about family members and their relationships over at least three generations. Many other symbols can be used besides the ones presented here.

Evans Family

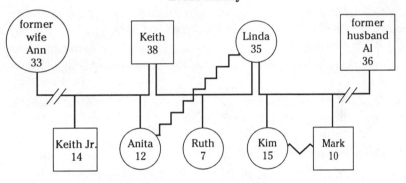

Symbols

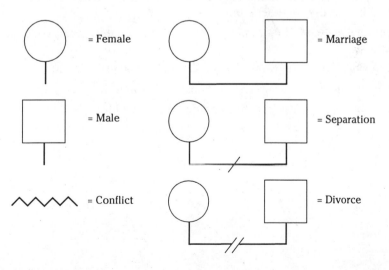

GUIDELINE

Group Leadership Skills

Source

Based on Corey, M. S., & Corey, G. (1987). *Groups: Process and practice* (3rd ed.). Pacific Grove, CA: Brooks/Cole.

Group leadership skills can be effectively applied to family therapy. These skills can also be taught to clients to use in their homes.

1. *Restating:* saying in slightly different words what a participant has said to clarify its meaning.

2. *Clarifying:* grasping the essence of a message at both the feeling and thinking levels. Clarifying simplifies a client's statements by focusing on the core of the message.

3. *Summarizing:* pulling together the important elements of an interaction or session.

4. *Confronting:* challenging individuals to look at discrepancies in words, nonverbals, and actions. Use "I" statements, a nonaccusatory tone, and concrete feedback.

5. *Reflecting:* presenting back to the client the client's feelings.

6. *Supporting:* providing encouragement and reinforcement.

7. *Goal setting:* planning specific goals for the group process.

8. *Giving feedback:* expressing concrete and honest reactions to and observations of a family member's behavior.

9. *Protecting:* safeguarding family members from unnecessary psychological risks.

10. *Disclosing oneself:* revealing one's reactions to events in the here and now.

11. *Modeling:* demonstrating desired behavior through actions.

12. *Blocking:* intervening to stop unproductive behavior.

GUIDELINE

Humor

Source

Based on Napier, R. W., & Gershenfeld, M. K. (1987). *Groups: Theory and experience.* Boston: Houghton Mifflin.

Family systems are complex, and within this complexity are numerous opportunities to cultivate humor. Have the family bring something funny to the dinner table or therapy session. For small children it could be a funny face, picture, or joke. Older children or adults should personalize the humor to their family by collecting funny stories, occurrences, or events in their lives.

Things to look for:

things that happened to you

paradoxes within the family

most unforgettable moments

irony

most forgettable moments

unanticipated events

occurrences

unpredictable events

universal truths

absurd situations

imagining how things will look twenty years from now

overdramatization

exaggeration

Things to avoid:

sarcasm

nasty biting wit

laughing at someone rather than with them

choking on your food!

GUIDELINE

Listening

Source
Excerpts from *Perceptive listening* (2nd ed.), by Florence I. Wolff and Nadine Marsnik. Copyright © 1992 Holt, Rinehart and Winston, Inc., used by permission of the publisher.

We all need to improve our listening skills, individually and in families. These techniques can help in this process.

1. *Listen with an open mind.* Family members must consider all sides of an issue before making decisions that affect the family.

2. *Listen and concentrate on the speaker's topic in order to stimulate interest.* Both parents and children have responsibility as speakers and listeners in the family. We must be interested in each other.

3. *Listen and adapt to the speaker's appearance, personality, and delivery.* Our attitudes make us react differently to people who are different from us, especially in families. Adapting to nonverbal cues lets us hear the content.

4. *Listen for concepts and central ideas instead of facts.* What individuals say to each other and what they imply provide insight for families. Listen to the big picture.

5. *Listen to curb and overcome distractions.* We need to control our reactions to many distractions. Focus on the speaker.

6. *Listen without faking attention or pretending to listen.* To pretend to listen is an attempt to deceive the other person. Be genuine.

7. *Listen to the entire message without judging or refuting.* Family members must listen to the whole message before responding to any part of it.

8. *Listen to unfamiliar and difficult material.* This is the hardest time to listen to another family member. It is also the most crucial time to listen.

9. *Listen to the silence.* Silence can be good if it gives family members time to think through what has been said. It can be bad if it's used to punish another family member.

GUIDELINE

Psychodrama

Source

Based on Blatner, M. D., & Blatner, A. (1988). *Foundations of psychodrama: History, theory, and practice.* New York: Springer.

Psychodrama can be used to rework past concerns, to work on current concerns, or to practice future confrontations. It can be used for all age groups, beginning with pre-kindergartners and extending to geriatric groups.

Traditional Psychodrama Roles

- *Director:* This is the person who facilitates the drama, usually the counselor.
- *Protagonist:* This is the principal role or the person who presents the issue.
- *Auxiliaries:* These are the persons or people who take on the roles of the other significant people in the protagonist's drama.

Other Definitions

- *Soliloquy:* The director and protagonist leave the scene and walk around it, looking at it, so that their thoughts about the situation can be expressed outside the confrontation.
- *Sharing:* The group, without giving advice, shares similar feelings or scenarios with the protagonist and group.
- *Doubling:* The double functions as support to the protagonist's feeling or position, often saying what the protagonist can't or won't say. Protagonists always should be encouraged to put the double's thoughts in their own words or to reject them if appropriate.

Things for the Director to Keep in Mind

- *Deal with the dramas as if they were happening in the present.*
- *Encourage physical action as opposed to talking about a situation.*
- *Use metaphor and encourage specificity as opposed to abstraction.*
- *Utilize the group and have fun.*

GUIDELINE

Reverse Role Playing

Source

From Davis, K. M. (1993). *Working with children*. Unpublished manuscript.

These guidelines provide an overview of the technique that can be shared with a person or family.

1. The goal of reverse role playing is to increase the person's awareness.
2. The person and counselor role-play the problem that has been identified.
3. The person and the counselor switch roles after the counselor has understood how the person deals with the problem.
4. The counselor may attempt to exaggerate the perceived affect.
5. The counselor can ask for clarification as the reverse role playing unfolds.
6. The counselor and the person improve the reverse role playing, to make their behavior seem even more realistic.
7. The person and counselor process the experience.
8. The counselor can help the person identify insights by sharing the feelings and thoughts that arose during the reverse role playing.

GUIDELINE

Role Playing

Source

From Davis, K. M. 1993. *Working with children.* Unpublished manuscript.

Role playing is a technique that can help clients explore, understand, and change themselves in a positive way. It can be used for decision making and exploring consequences and can lead to solutions.

1. The goal of this technique is to increase the counselor's awareness.
2. The counselor helps the person explore issues that identify a significant problem.
3. The person recalls a specific situation in which the problem has occurred.
4. The person will role-play their part in the conflict.
5. The person tells the counselor what his or her role will be.
6. The counselor role-plays the other person involved in the conflict.
7. The person and the counselor attempt to re-create the situation through role playing.
8. The person and counselor process experience and make corrections to determine the thoughts and feelings that impact the situation.
9. The person and the counselor repeat role-play until the situation is depicted accurately.

GUIDELINE

Self-Disclosure

Source

Based on Johnson, D. W. (1993). *Reaching out* (5th ed.). Boston: Allyn & Bacon.

Good self-disclosure requires the following:

1. The individual is aware of his or her feelings, thoughts, and individual personal reactions toward others.
2. The individual speaks in the first person, using "I" statements when self-disclosing.
3. The individual makes a statement rather than asks a question.
4. The individual does not blame others for making him or her angry, sad, hurt, or jealous. The individual simply states how he or she feels.
5. The individual makes appropriate, concrete, and specific disclosures.
6. The goal of self-disclosure is to facilitate honesty and authenticity—to help, not hurt.

GUIDELINE

Skeleton Keys

Source

Based on de Shazer, S. (1985). *Keys to the solution in brief therapy.* New York: Norton.

Write/Read/Burn

Starting on the day after this session, a person who holds a bitterness toward a spouse will write down all the bad experiences and all the good experiences the person remembers. The next day the person will read and then burn what he or she wrote. The person will alternate days until the next session. The major purpose of this intervention is to help someone release bitterness about a relationship.

Structured Fight

Instruct the couple to toss a coin to decide who will begin the structured fight. The winner then gets to complain for the first ten minutes without any interruptions. The other person is then allowed ten minutes to complain without any interruptions. Ten minutes of silence by both parties follow. If there is more to argue about, the couple tosses the coin again to decide who begins the second round. The major reason for implementing this intervention is to help the couple establish new patterns of decision making and communication.

Do Something Different

The therapist gives a person in the family an idea of how to do something different from what the person has been doing to deal with a specific problem. The idea can come from the therapist, and the change should occur before the next session. The value in this technique is that the therapy becomes part of the solution, and the person begins to learn how to internalize change.

Overcoming the Urge

A person in the family is directed to observe the compulsive behavior they struggle with carefully. The person then needs to make very concrete and specific observations about what they are doing when they overcome or resist the compulsion. These observations are then discussed in detail. The intervention is based on the rationale that success tends to feed on success.

GUIDELINE

Stances

Source
> Based on Satir, V. (1972). *Peoplemaking.* Palo Alto, CA: Science & Behavior Books.

1. Identify each stance (blamer, placator, computer, distractor).
2. Identify any stances you recognize in your family.

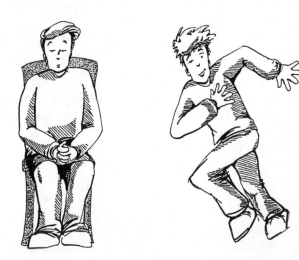

GUIDELINE

Time Out

Source

Based on Granvold, D. K. (1994). *Cognitive and behavioral treatment methods and applications*. Pacific Grove, CA: Brooks/Cole.

Time out is one method parents may use to reinforce desirable behaviors and weaken undesirable behaviors in their children. A time out is a short period of isolation (five minutes for young children, fifteen minutes for older ones) in which the parent or parents send the child to a nonstimulating room, such as the living room, dining room, or bathroom. The child must refrain from the undesirable behavior during the entire time-out period.

- The therapist should determine which types of behavior qualify for time outs.
- Select an appropriate time-out room or rooms.
- Know at what point in the situation to call for a time out. (Trust your judgment.)
- Explain to the child what a time out is.
- Children should know what behavior is desirable and undesirable.
- Parental commands and requests must be clearly expressed to the child.
- A time-out warning may be given to the child as an incentive to change his or her behavior.
- Call for a time out by simply telling the child to take a time out for a specified period of time.
- After a time out is called, do not discuss the situation with the child.
- The child will interpret any conversation as attention.
- Attention is generally viewed in a positive light and may reinforce the undesirable behavior.
- If needed, the parent may physically take the child to the time out room.
- The child may leave the time out room and rejoin the family's activity once the time is over.
- It is important to be consistent in giving time outs.

WORKSHEET

Anger

Source

Based on Carter, L., & Minirth, F. (1993). *The anger workbook*. Nashville: Thomas Nelson.

This worksheet helps identify the *why, what,* and *how* behind your anger. Complete the following statements.

1. I get angry when . . . _____

_____

_____

_____

2. My anger becomes physical when . . . _____

_____

_____

_____

3. When others vent their anger on me I feel . . . _____

_____

_____

_____

4. My childhood memories of anger are . . . _____

_____

_____

_____

5. After I get angry, I feel . . . _____

_____

_____

_____

6. I can handle my anger better by . . . _____

_____

_____

_____

7. I need to work with _____

_____ to better handle my anger.

WORKSHEET

Caring Days

Source

Based on Stuart, R. (1980). *Helping couples change: A social learning approach to marital therapy.* New York: Guilford Press.

During the next week, list ten behaviors of your spouse that show your spouse loves you. You should have a his and hers list and try to do at least five of them each week. Once your list is completed, show it to your spouse, and ask him or her to demonstrate at least five of these behaviors each day.

Behavior Showing Love

1. _____
   _____

2. _____
   _____

3. _____
   _____

4. _____
   _____

5. _____
   _____

6. _____
   _____

7. _____
   _____

8. _____
   _____

9. _____
   _____

10. _____
    _____

WORKSHEET

Childhood Memory

Source
From Davis, K. (1993). *Childhood memory.* Unpublished manuscript.

The purpose of this worksheet is to help you recall life experiences and events.

- Describe everything you recall about the setting.
- Describe how you felt both emotionally and physically.
- Describe what happened after the event. What were the emotional, mental, physical, and relationship consequences?

Time—season: _____ Year: _____

Place: _____

Who was present? _____

_____

_____

_____

_____

Describe the setting: _____

_____

_____

_____

Describe your feelings: _____

_____

_____

_____

_____

Describe the outcome: _____

_____

_____

_____

_____

WORKSHEET

Communication Roadblocks

Source

Based on Thompson, C. L., & Rudolph, L. B. (1992). *Counseling children* (3rd ed.). Pacific Grove, CA: Brooks/Cole.

The following worksheet is divided into seven response categories. For each category, the first part comprises two examples of things people say that create roadblocks to effective communication. The second part allows the client to write his or her own examples of responses that create roadblocks.

Evaluation Responses

1. Examples: (a) You are wrong to get angry at your spouse. (b) You never spend quality time with the children.

2. Client's example: _____

   _____

Advice-Giving Responses

1. Examples: (a) Why don't you try to be more understanding with your spouse? (b) My advice is to count to ten before you discipline your children.

2. Client's example: _____

   _____

Helping Response, or One-Upmanship

1. Examples: (a) That's nothing; when I was a kid I had to walk five miles to school with holes in my shoes. (b) You had shoes?

2. Client's example: _____

   _____

Diagnosing, Psychoanalytic Responses

1. Examples: (a) Why do you feel so unhappy? It is because you are disappointed in yourself for not being a better husband and father. (b) How can you better communicate with your children?

2. Client's example: _____

   _____

Warning, Admonishing, Commanding Responses

1. Examples: (a) You had better start doing your homework when I tell you! (b) If you don't do as I say, you'll be grounded for the week!

2. Client's example: _____

   _____

Logical, Lecturing Responses

1. Examples: (a) If you persist in yelling at your children, rather than calmly disciplining them, they will eventually become frightened of you. (b) The fact is that your father's treatment of you has caused you to withdraw.
2. Client's example: _____

_____

Devaluation Responses

1. Examples: (a) It's not so bad—many fathers have a hard time communicating with their children. (b) You don't really hate your parents because of their disciplining methods.
2. Client's example: _____

_____

WORKSHEET

Conflict Resolution

Source

Based on Dinkmeyer, D., & Carlson, J. (1984). *Time for a better marriage.* Circle Pines, MN: American Guidance Service.

In relationships, conflict develops when one person's behavior does not match the other's expectations. Poor communication often sustains the conflict. Conflict may center on areas such as money, sex, work, children, friends, and recreation.

The following steps represent an effective process to resolve conflict. In the space provided, write ways in which you *do not* and you *do* demonstrate the behavior involved in the step.

1. Show mutual respect.
   I *do not* show respect to my spouse by _____

   _____

   _____

   _____

   I *do* show respect to my spouse by _____

   _____

   _____

   _____

2. Pinpoint the real issue.
   I *do not* share the real issue when _____

   _____

   _____

   _____

   I *do* share the real issue when _____

   _____

   _____

   _____

3. Seek areas of agreement.
   I *do not* seek areas of agreement by _____

   _____

   _____

   _____

I *do* seek areas of agreement by _____

_____

_____

_____

4. Mutually participate in decisions.
   We *do not* mutually participate in decisions when _____

   _____

   _____

   _____

   We *do* mutually participate in decisions when _____

   _____

   _____

   _____

WORKSHEET

Defining the Problem

Source

Based on Cormier, L. S., & Hackney, H. (1987). *The professional counselor: A process guide to helping.* Englewood Cliffs, NJ: Prentice-Hall.

Defining the problem is an integral part of effective family therapy. Each family member needs to participate in the defining process. In the four blocks below, each family member should supply the following information: Define the problem nondefensively in block one. State the problem in behavioral language in block two. Write the most troublesome part of the problem in block three. Describe what has been done to solve the problem in block four.

1. Nondefensive definition	2. Behavioral description
3. Most troublesome part	4. Past attempts to solve

WORKSHEET

Dimensions of Support

Source

Based on Pearson, R. E. (1982). Support: Exploration of a basic dimension of informal help and counseling. *Personnel and Guidance Journal, 61*(2), 83–87.

This worksheet asks you to state brief examples of how you demonstrate each of the ten support dimensions. Give examples of how you demonstrate each type of support for your spouse, children, or parent(s). Use the back of this sheet or another piece of paper if you need more room.

1. *Admiration:* Showing what you like about them.

   _____

2. *Love:* Putting others' needs above your own.

   _____

3. *Intimacy:* Being with others, hugging.

   _____

4. *Companionship:* Being together in the same area.

   _____

5. *Encouragement:* Being confident in others' abilities.

   _____

6. *Acceptance:* Understanding where others are at.

   _____

7. *Comfort:* Meeting others' needs.

   _____

8. *Help:* Doing things for and with others.

   _____

9. *Honesty:* Speaking truthfully.

   _____

10. *Caring:* Doing without asking.

    _____

WORKSHEET

Expectations

Source

Based on Stevens, J. O. (1981). *Awareness: Exploring, experimenting, experiencing.* New York: Bantam.

The purpose of this worksheet is to help family members clarify the family relationship expectations that they have for themselves and one another. Write down the expectations that you have for each family member in the appropriate area.

Person	Mother	Father	Sibling 1	Sibling 2
Mother	self			
Father		self		
Sibling 1			self	
Sibling 2				self

WORKSHEET

Family Minutes

Source

Based on Grunwald, B. B., & McAbee, H. (1985). *Guiding the family: Practical counseling techniques.* Muncie, IN: Accelerated Development.

Meeting Arrangements

Date: _____

Place: _____

Time: _____

Family Members Present

_____

_____

_____

_____

_____

_____

Issues Discussed

1. _____
   _____

2. _____
   _____

3. _____
   _____

Roadblocks or Stalemates

_____

_____

_____

_____

Family Decisions

_____

_____

_____

_____

Feelings (parents' reflections about the meeting)

_____

_____

_____

_____

WORKSHEET

Family Reconstruction

Source
Based on Satir, V., & Baldwin, M. (1983). *Satir step by step: A guide to creating change in families.* Palo Alto, CA: Science & Behavior Books.

Each family member should draw a map of the family, a family history, and a circle of influence. Each member needs three sheets of paper. Bring your information to the next session.

1. Map: at least two generations (see example)

Evans Family

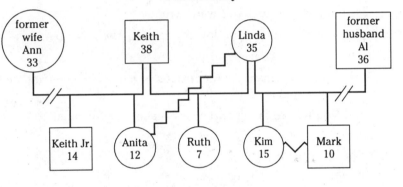

Symbols: ─/─ divorce ⋁⋀ conflict

2. Family history: mother, father, children

   How did the family start? _____

   _____

   _____

   Dates of important events: _____

   _____

   _____

3. To draw a circle of influence, draw a wheel with you at the center and each spoke leading to a family member. The thicker the spoke, the greater the influence that member has on you.

WORKSHEET

Forgiveness

Source

Based on Augsburger, D. (1981). *Caring enough to forgive, caring enough to not forgive.* Scottdale, PA: Herald Press.

Forgiveness is defined as giving up resentment or the desire to punish. When is forgiveness appropriate, and when is it not? Check off any of the following that personally involve you.

When to Forgive

Do you forgive . . .

_____ 1. When you realize that you were wronged?

_____ 2. When you realize that you love or care for the other person(s)?

_____ 3. By letting go of the past?

_____ 4. When you realize that the other person is genuinely repentant and has learned a lesson?

_____ 5. When you realize the importance of family and community?

When Not to Forgive

Do you refrain from forgiving . . .

_____ 1. When forgiveness puts you in a one-up (better than the other) position?

_____ 2. Without telling the intended person of your forgiveness?

_____ 3. Without first expressing your feelings of pain, hurt, anger, or embarrassment?

_____ 4. When you feel you aren't going to continue a relationship with the other person?

WORKSHEET

Johari Window

Source

Adapted from Luft, J. (1969). *Of human interaction*. Palo Alto, CA: National Press. Adapted with permission of the author.

The Johari window is a tool that helps a person understand how feedback and self-disclosure can help one to gain greater self-awareness, and help others to know one better.

Feedback ⟶

		Things Known to Self	Things Unknown to Self
S **e** **l** **f** **-** **D** **i** **s** **c** **l** **o** **s** **u** **r** **e**	Things known to others	**Public Area** information known both to yourself and others	**Blind Area** information about yourself that others know, but that you are unable to see
	Things unknown to others	**Hidden Area** information you know about yourself but keep hidden from others	**The Unknown Self**

As feedback from others increases, the public area gets larger and the blind area gets smaller. The person becomes more known to him- or herself. As the person engages in more self-disclosure, the public area pushes into the hidden area. The person becomes more known to others. On a separate sheet of paper, write down everything you can do to increase the areas in which you are known to yourself and to others.

WORKSHEET

Journal Format

Source

Based on Deetz, S. A., & Stevenson, S. L. (1986). *Managing interpersonal communications.* New York: Harper & Row.

This chart contains space for one week of keeping a journal. Briefly write positive and negative feelings, thoughts, actions, and events for the corresponding day. Carry a small notepad when away from home so you can jot down your reactions.

Day	Positive	Negative
Monday		
Tuesday		
Wednesday		
Thursday		
Friday		
Saturday		
Sunday		

WORKSHEET

Marriage Model

Source

Based on Haley, J. (1963). Marriage therapy. *Archives of General Psychiatry,* *8*(3), 213–234.

This exercise will help you become aware of your beliefs about marriage. Think about the one marriage (other than your own) that has had the greatest influence on your life. You will share and compare your beliefs with those of your spouse. You may select the marriage of parents, grandparents, uncles, aunts, close neighbors, or others.

What did the man do best and worst for the marriage?

Best: _____

_____

Worst: _____

_____

What did the woman do best and worst for the marriage?

_____

Best: _____

_____

Worst: _____

_____

Who was in charge of the relationship? _____

_____

How did they say no to each other? _____

_____

How did they handle and resolve conflicts? _____

_____

How did they avoid or assume responsibility for conflicts? _____

_____

What was their style of being affectionate? _____

_____

How does your marriage resemble this model? What are the similarities and the differences? How might your own behavior be improved? _____

_____

WORKSHEET

Meta-Rules

Source

Based on Haley, J. (1963). Marriage therapy. *Archives of General Psychiatry,*
8(3), 213–234.

Rules about making, setting, and enforcing rules are called meta-rules.
Make a list of the rules that you compiled on the worksheet about rules (see
page 267). Add the following symbols after each rule:

A, if both partners agree to the rule
D, if the partners disagree
H, if the husband originated the rule
W, if the wife originated the rule
h, if the husband enforces the rule
w, if the wife enforces the rule

You may want to recopy the rules onto another sheet of paper and add col-
umns for the symbols. From this list, answer the following questions as best
you can.

1. Who sets the rules in your family? Does one partner set rules in some areas
   and the other partner in other areas? _____
   _____
   _____

2. What are some meta-rules in your marriage? _____
   _____
   _____

3. Who enforces the rules? How? _____
   _____
   _____

4. What happens when partners disagree on a rule? _____
   _____
   _____

5. How might you resolve family arguments in the future, taking your meta-
   rules into account? _____
   _____
   _____

WORKSHEET

Monitoring

Source

Based on Lange, A., & Hart, D. (1983). *Directive family therapy.* New York: Brunner/Mazel.

This worksheet is designed to assist a couple or family to develop self-awareness and to understand what it is they want from one another. This worksheet should be completed as soon as an incident occurs.

Date: _____

Time: _____

Place: _____

Brief description: _____

_____

_____

_____

_____

_____

How did the incident make you feel? _____

_____

_____

_____

_____

_____

What exactly did you want for the other to do? _____

_____

_____

_____

_____

_____

WORSHEET

Nonverbal Cues

Source

Based on Deetz, S. A., & Stevenson, S. L. (1986). *Managing interpersonal communication*. New York: Harper & Row.

Interpersonal communication involves the use of nonverbal messages and cues. A clear understanding of inflections, gestures, and expressions is necessary to communicate with others effectively. Check off the nonverbal cues you receive from the other person.

[ ] Keeping hands open	[ ] Buttoning coat or drawing away
[ ] Unbuttoning coat	[ ] Sitting on edge of chair
[ ] Crossing arms on chest	[ ] Unbuttoning coat
[ ] Crossing legs	[ ] Tilting head
[ ] Making gestures with a fist	[ ] Clearing throat
[ ] Pointing index finger	[ ] Whistling
[ ] Pinching flesh	[ ] Smoking cigarettes
[ ] Chewing pen or pencil	[ ] Fidgeting in chair
[ ] Rubbing thumb over thumb	[ ] Not looking at other person
[ ] Biting fingernails	[ ] Jingling money in pockets
[ ] Holding hands in a steepled position	[ ] Tugging at ear
[ ] Putting hands behind back	[ ] Stroking chin
[ ] Stiffening back	[ ] Peering over glasses
[ ] Putting hands in pockets with thumbs out	[ ] Cleaning glasses
[ ] Crossing arms	[ ] Chewing on glasses
[ ] Glancing sideways	[ ] Taking short breaths
[ ] Touching or rubbing nose	[ ] Glaring at others
[ ] Rubbing eyes	[ ] Turning away from others
[ ] Wringing hands	[ ] Daydreaming
[ ] Pouting	[ ] Crying

Other behaviors you have noticed:

How did it make you feel when you noticed the nonverbal cue?

WORKSHEET

Observation

Source

Based on Borich, G. D. (1990). *Observation skills for effective teaching.* Columbus, OH: Merrill Publishing.

Observation, within a family or a relationship, is the condition of accurately noticing interactions.

The following list represents social dimensions that impact on relationships. Write the number *1* next to the item if too much of that dimension appears in your relationship, and the number *2* if too little of the dimension appears. The number *3* represents the appropriate amount.

____ *Cohesiveness:* a feeling of intimacy, connection, and togetherness resulting from genuine interaction

____ *Diversity:* a constructive and appropriate level of different interests and goals in the relationship or the family

____ *Formality:* rules, guidelines, and consistent ways of behaving that provide a positive grounding in the relationship

____ *Pace:* how individuals in a relationship are willing and able to adjust their life pace to accommodate the pace of the other member of the relationship

____ *Good communication:* how individual goals are stated in the relationship

____ *Favoritism:* how an individual shows bias or favoritism toward another person

____ *Taking sides:* how a person takes sides either for or against another

____ *Satisfaction:* how an individual is satisfied in the relationship

____ *Organization:* how an individual experiences order, stability, and support in the relationship

____ *Difficulty:* how an individual feels and thinks the relationship is difficult

____ *Enthusiasm:* how a person is hopeful, positive, and excited about the relationship

____ *Fairness:* how an individual is just, fair, and evenhanded

---

WORKSHEET

Obstacles Analysis

Source
Based on Nelson-Jones, R. (1993). *Student manual for lifeskills helping.* Pacific Grove, CA: Brooks/Cole.

This worksheet is designed to help people examine specific obstacles they encounter during the problem-solving process. The person is asked to write down specific parts of the problem-solving process. The person then records corresponding self-statements, fears, beliefs, feelings, and outcomes.

Parts of the Situation	Self-Statements	My Fears
Example: I need to get a job.	Example: It's hard to get a job.	Example: I will never get a job.
My Beliefs	**My Feeling**	**Possible Outcomes**
Example: It will take a long time.	Example: I am impatient.	Example: I will get a job in time.

WORKSHEET

Pathway

Source

Based on Minuchin, S., Montalvo, B., Guerney, B., Rosman, B., & Schumer, F. (1976). *Families of the slum.* New York: Basic Books.

---

1. *Identified pathway:* The therapist gives his or her perceptions of the steps the family takes along the pathway. Describe as many characteristics of the pathway as possible.

   a. _____ e. _____

   _____ _____

   b. _____ f. _____

   _____ _____

   c. _____ g. _____

   _____ _____

   d. _____ h. _____

   _____ _____

---

2. *Choices:* The pathway is discussed by the family, along with each of the following alternatives.

   [ ] Follow existing pathway: _____

   _____

   _____

   [ ] Disobey, indirectly: _____

   _____

   _____

   [ ] Disobey, directly: _____

   _____

   _____

   [ ] Eliminate pathway: _____

   _____

   _____

WORKSHEET

Problem Solving

Source
Based on Haley, J. (1987). *Problem-solving therapy.* San Francisco: Jossey-Bass.

This worksheet is designed to help clients examine the activities and obstacles involved in attempting to solve a particular problem. Clients are asked to select a recent problem and to record the activities that took place and the obstacles they encountered in various categories.

Stages	Activities	Obstacles
Defining the problem		
Coming up with alternatives		
Choosing one alternative		
Acting on that alternative		
Evaluating		

WORKSHEET

Quid pro Quo Cards

Source

Based on Jackson, D. D. (1977). Family rules: Marital quid pro quo. In P. Watzlawick & J. H. Weakland (Eds.), *The interactional view: Studies at the Mental Research Institute, Palo Alto, 1965–74.* New York: Norton.

Use the following boxes to create four individual cards (perhaps by photocopying this page and cutting out the squares). Distribute the cards to each family member. Then, follow the procedures outlined in the quid pro quo technique in Part Two.

_____ , I want/need you to: What: When: For how long? Initials: _____ _____	_____ I want/need you to: What: When: For how long? Initials: _____ _____
_____ , I want/need you to: What: When: For how long? Initials: _____ _____	_____ I want/need you to: What: When: For how long? Initials: _____ _____

WORKSHEET

Relabeling

Source

Based on Minuchin, S. (1974). *Families and family therapy.* Cambridge, MA: Harvard University Press.

Negative Message	Positive Message
I am very upset with you.	I really care about you.

Write a negative message in the left column and then, with the entire family, write an alternative message that is positive.

WORSHEET

Rules

Source

Based on Haley, J. (1963). Marriage therapy. *Archives of General Psychiatry,* *8*(3), 213–234.

Early in a relationship, couples begin establishing rules that are expressed both overtly and covertly. The purpose of this exercise is to help you become aware of the overt and covert rules in your marriage. Try to write two rules in each category below. Write *O* after the rule if it is an overt rule. Write *C* after the rule if it is a covert rule.

Work: _____

_____

_____

Social life: _____

_____

_____

Money: _____

_____

_____

Sex: _____

_____

_____

Communication: _____

_____

_____

Roles: _____

_____

_____

Families of origin: _____

_____

_____

After identifying these rules, you may want to keep, revise, or discard them according to your present needs.

WORKSHEET

Simple Contract

Source

Based on Wolfgang, C. H., & Glickman, C. D. (1986). *Solving discipline problems: Strategies for classroom teaching* (2nd ed.). Boston: Allyn & Bacon.

Name: _____

Date: _____

Time frame: _____

Goals of the contract

Short term: _____

_____

_____

_____

Long term: _____

_____

_____

_____

_____

Action steps: _____

_____

_____

_____

_____

Rewards: _____

_____

_____

_____

_____

1st person   _____
                              (signature)

2nd person   _____
                              (signature)

WORKSHEET

Telegrams

Source

Based on Stevens, J. O. (1981). *Awareness: Exploring, experimenting, experiencing.* New York: Bantam.

EASTERN ONION TELEGRAM

From: _____

To: _____

Message: _____

_____

_____

_____

_____

_____

_____

The Quickest, Surest Way to Communicate

EASTERN ONION TELEGRAM

From: _____

To: _____

Message: _____

_____

_____

_____

_____

_____

The Quickest, Surest Way to Communicate

WORKSHEET

Time Cable

Source

Based on Hoffman, L. (1983). Diagnosis and assessment in family therapy: II. A co-evolutionary framework for systemic family therapy. *Family Therapy Collections, 4,* 35–61. Rockville, MD: Aspen Systems.

The time cable helps each family member examine the presenting problem from the perspectives of past, present, and future. In the spaces provided below, discuss the problem within the time frame categories. If you need more space, use a separate sheet of paper.

Background: _____

_____

_____

_____

_____

When problem began: _____

_____

_____

_____

_____

Present: _____

_____

_____

_____

_____

_____

Future: _____

_____

_____

_____

_____

_____

_____

WORKSHEET

Typical Day Journal

Source

Based on Grunwald, B. B., & McAbee, H. M. (1985). *Guiding the family: Practical counseling techniques.* Muncie, IN: Accelerated Development.

Keep a detailed observation record by relating at least two events that occur while you are involved in each of the following.

I. Getting up

Action by	Reaction	Goal
1. _____	1. _____	1. _____
2. _____	2. _____	2. _____

II. Mealtimes

1. _____	1. _____	1. _____
2. _____	2. _____	2. _____

III. Watching TV

1. _____	1. _____	1. _____
2. _____	2. _____	2. _____

IV. Homework

1. _____	1. _____	1. _____
2. _____	2. _____	2. _____

V. Chores

1. _____	1. _____	1. _____
2. _____	2. _____	2. _____

VI. Recreation

1. _____	1. _____	1. _____
2. _____	2. _____	2. _____

VII. Bedtime

1. _____	1. _____	1. _____
2. _____	2. _____	2. _____

WORKSHEET

Vulnerability Contract

Source

Based on Duhl, B. S. (1976). *The vulnerability contract: A tool for turning alienation into connection with couples, families, and groups.* Mexico City: First International Family Encounter.

Wife: _____ Husband: _____ Child: _____

Worst times (Identify a specific incident):

1. _____

2. _____

Self-awareness (How do I know there is a problem?):

1. _____

2. _____

Others' awareness (How do others know there is a problem?):

1. _____

2. _____

AGREEMENT

When _____ tells me the above, I, _____ will:

1. _____

2. _____

Agreed _____ _____ _____
        Signature of wife   Signature of husband   Signature of child

Have each individual complete the above independently and then share with the others.

Epilogue

The Evans family members have begun to examine the different roles and rules they have collected through their past family experiences. By exploring their individual issues, the Evans have a much clearer picture of themselves as a family.

Areas of conflict continue to exist. Now, however, through an understanding of the emotional connections involved in areas of conflict, change is facilitated. Change is the ultimate goal of family counseling—change of overt or covert expectations, roles, rules, and perceived needs. The Evans family is well on its way to healthy interaction. Family members' conflicts are by no means over, but they now have the tools with which to build a closer, more meaningful family environment.

Brooks/Cole Publishing is dedicated to publishing fine books for the helping professions. If you would like to learn more about our publications, please use this mailer to request our catalogue.

Name: _____

Street Address: _____

City, State, Zip Code: _____

FOLD HERE

BUSINESS REPLY MAIL
FIRST CLASS   PERMIT NO. 358   PACIFIC GROVE, CA

POSTAGE WILL BE PAID BY ADDRESSEE

ATT: *Human Services Catalogue*

**Brooks/Cole Publishing Company
511 Forest Lodge Road
Pacific Grove, California 93950-9968**

FOLD HERE

TO THE OWNER OF THIS BOOK

We hope that you have found *Families: A Handbook of Concepts and Techniques for the Helping Professional* useful. So that this book can be improved in a future edition, would you take the time to complete this sheet and return it? Thank you.

School and address: ——————————————————————————————————————

Department: ——————————————————————————————————————

Instructor's name: ——————————————————————————————————————

1. What I like most about this book is: ——————————————————————

——

——

2. What I like least about this book is: ——————————————————————

——

——

3. My general reaction to this book is: ——————————————————————

——

4. The name of the course in which I used this book is: ————————————

——

5. In the space below, or on a separate sheet of paper, please write specific suggestions for improving this book and anything else you'd care to share about your experience in using the book.

——

——

——

——

——

Optional

Your name: _____ Date: _____

May Brooks/Cole quote you, either in promotion for *Families: A Handbook of Concepts and Techniques for the Helping Professional* or in future publishing ventures?

    Yes: _____ No: _____

    Sincerely,

    Kenneth Davis

FOLD HERE

- -

NO POSTAGE
NECESSARY
IF MAILED
IN THE
UNITED STATES

BUSINESS REPLY MAIL

FIRST CLASS   PERMIT NO. 358   PACIFIC GROVE, CA

POSTAGE WILL BE PAID BY ADDRESSEE

ATT: *Kenneth Davis* _____

Brooks/Cole Publishing Company
511 Forest Lodge Road
Pacific Grove, California 93950-9968

FOLD HERE